CONTENTS

PART ONE:

In the Family

Unit
1

AMINA
Shirley Saad

The Middle East

Unit
2

EVERY LIGHT IN THE
HOUSE BURNIN'
Andrea Levy

Jamaica
and the United Kingdom

Unit
3

FAMILY ALBUM
Siv Cedering

Sweden

Unit
4

THE VISIT
Catherine Lim

Singapore

Unit
5

SPRING LOVE
Mia Yun

Korea

PART TWO:
Into Adulthood

PART THREE:
Culture Clash

Unit
11

THINGS FALL APART
Chinua Achebe

Nigeria

Unit
12

LOOKING FOR A RAIN GOD
Bessie Head

Botswana

Unit
13

CRICKETS
Robert Olen Butler

Vietnam
and the USA

Unit
14

A FAMILY SUPPER
Kazuo Ishiguro

Japan

INTRODUCTION

WHAT IS *VIEWS AND VOICES?*

Views and Voices: Writers of English Around the World is an answer to requests by numerous teachers for an anthology of writings by authors whose first language is English, but whose first culture is not. Some authors we have chosen are, in fact, bicultural. We have carefully selected stories, or excerpts from novels, that will engage students intellectually and emotionally, and that are accessible to the average student above the age of sixteen. Whereas most collections of literary excerpts are geared towards the advanced-level EFL, ESL, and English student in college or university, *Views and Voices* is aimed at intermediate-level students at high school, college, university, or an institution of adult education. It is intended for those students who have achieved a good grasp of grammar and basic vocabulary and now need to enhance their command of English to express themselves in progressively more complex ways. The book has been designed with flexibility in mind and, as such, can be successfully used in a conventional classroom as well as in tutoring and distance-learning programs. It is particularly suited for international students, but could also be used by Anglo-American students who are interested in getting to know the wider world.

The following outstanding characteristics distinguish this book from others:

- ⊘ Each reading is an authentic literary selection authored by an international writer whose dominant language is English, but whose culture transcends national boundaries.
- ⊘ The emotionally and intellectually engaging readings and activities appeal to both ESL and EFL students around the world.
- ⊘ Each unit offers a special section of Internet activities and online resources.
- ⊘ The readings are preceded and followed by exercises on vocabulary, "language chunks," language style, and language variety.
- ⊘ Recap questions are presented within the reading selections.
- ⊘ All activities are suitable for inclusion in a portfolio.

WHY *VIEWS AND VOICES?*

Many teachers today are aware of the controversy surrounding the growth of English and its effects on other languages and cultures around the globe. Robert Phillipson, in his book *Linguistic Imperialism*

(1992), asserts that the spread of English is a positive force that need not be accompanied by the imposition of Anglo-American culture and hegemony. One way of avoiding the kind of cultural imperialism that Phllipson and others are concerned about is to have students read works by international authors who write about their own worlds in English.

Students of English who are not from the major English speaking countries find this kind of literature appealing. In the lesson "Multicultural Ideas" in *New Ways of Using Drama and Literature in Language Teaching,* I noted that "By reading books that allow them to concentrate on the story development for which they possess the schema, students are less frustrated than when they have to try to understand both the language and the culture" (Whiteson 1996, 58). Often, students do not possess the contextual framework they need to read mainstream American and British writers such as Arthur Miller and Jane Austen without a struggle. Writers like Anita Desai, Chinua Achebe, and Catherine Lim, on the other hand, deal with transnational themes and use language that is more accessible both to ESL and EFL students.

Since the Civil Rights Movement, educators in the United States have sought to diversify reading lists by including texts by writers of various minority groups now recognized as integral to the American ground—African Americans, Asian Americans, Latin Americans, and Native Americans. With this volume, we are seeking to enlarge the concept of literary diversity by introducing students to international voices that are rarely, if ever, included in American textbooks. In doing so, we hope to showcase a literature that is prolific, varied, and largely unknown. Chinua Achebe, referring to the African writer, says, "He should aim at fashioning out an English which is at once universal and able to carry his peculiar experience." We believe that the authors we have selected embody this stance.

WHAT ARE THE STORIES IN *VIEWS AND VOICES?*

The focus of *Views and Voices* is primarily on the enjoyment of reading literature. There is an old adage that says that studying literature is good for one's general personal development; it makes one a well-rounded human being. There is no doubt that the study of literature encourages imagination and creativity. Herbert Marcuse, the philosopher, writes, "Art cannot change the world, but it can contribute to changing the consciousness and drives of the men and women who could change the world." This book is an attempt to open new vistas for students, to offer a taste of other cultures, and to entertain new points of view.

Views and Voices contains fourteen units divided into three sections: *Part One: In the Family*, *Part Two: Into Adulthood*, and *Part Three: Culture Clash*.

The five stories in the first section center on how individuals observe and are defined by their parents and extended family. The first story, "Amina," deals with childbirth and cultural issues. "Every Light in the House Burnin'" paints a wistful portrait of a young woman's parents. In "Family Album," the narrator acknowledges the importance and influence of the family members who preceded her. The departure of a mother has a terrible effect on a small child in "The Visit"; finally, "Spring Love" describes a young girl's first venture into relations between men and women.

The five stories in the second section cover five very different young lives. In "Fasting, Feasting," parental needs confine a young woman in child-like dependency; in "Poor Visitor," the narrator suffers the pangs of culture shock and homesickness. "About the Wedding Feast" underlines the generational and cultural gaps in an African family, and in "Clothes," we share a pivotal moment in a young wife's life. Finally, "Second Class Citizen" portrays a bold strike for identity and recognition.

The last section of the book recognizes the thorny problems that can characterize the meetings of cultures. In "Things Fall Apart" and "Looking for a Rain God," cultural misunderstandings and lack of acceptance reign. In "Crickets," a father is unable to pass on even a slender thread of his culture to his son. In the final story, "A Family Supper," a family gathers to "digest" their differences.

The stories have been chosen to inspire students to want to write or speak about their own worlds. However you integrate these stories into your existing curriculum, may they succeed in giving you a meaningful journey through the world of *Views and Voices!*

VW

Philipson, R. 1992. *Linguistic Imperialism*. Oxford: Oxford University Press.
Whiteson, V. 1996. *New Ways of Using Drama and Literature in Language Teaching*. Alexandria, VA. TESOL.

HOW TO USE THIS BOOK

Views and Voices features fourteen stories, or extracts from novels, that deal with different cultures. Naturally, we could not cover the whole world. The following section offers information and suggestions to assist you in using *Views and Voices* with your students. A typical unit has the following structure:

PRE-READING ACTIVITIES AND THE STORY

Introduction: These five to eight questions are designed to activate the student's schema, provide background information, and focus attention on the main topic in the story. These questions can be a warm-up for the whole class or discussed in small groups. Alternatively, they could be used for a chat room or email activity. The questions work as pre-reading organizers for understanding the story.

Library/Internet Tasks: These pre-reading tasks are especially suitable for students studying outside a conventional classroom, but can also be assigned as homework prior to reading the text. They not only reinforce students' research and technical skills, but they provide sufficient background information for comprehending the reading's context.

The Story: Each story is preceded by a brief paragraph of information about the author. The story is then presented in sections with key *vocabulary* defined and numerous sets of *recapitulation questions:*

⊘ **Vocabulary** that may present problems is glossed in the margins of the story pages on which it appears. The bold words are considered to be level-appropriate for intermediate readers and should be learned; the numbered words are for understanding the text. Rather than offering lengthy definitions, we provide the student with words or phrases that are synonymous. Whether a word is to be considered beginning, intermediate, or advanced is to some extent a judgement call based on the author's personal and professional experience. Still, a standard was needed to justify our decisions and we followed *Longman's Dictionary of Contemporary English* (2000) useful classification of frequency of usage as our guide. However, individual teachers and their students must, in the end, opt for what serves their needs best and make amendments whenever necessary.

⊘ **Recapitulation questions** within the text should be used on a "need only" basis. Their purpose is to help the student understand the text and to move on to the next section as seamlessly as possible since interruptions lessen both comprehension and the pleasure of reading. Depending on the comprehension level of students, teachers can elect whether to use these questions or not.

POST-READING ACTIVITIES AND FURTHER EXPLORATION

The exercises and activities that follow the story have been designed with flexibility in mind, so they can be easily used in a variety of teaching environments. Depending on the specific needs of students, they can be used to reinforce writing, speaking, or listening skills. They can be completed individually, in pairs or small groups, in the classroom, or using emails or chat rooms. They can also be assigned for homework. They fall into the following categories:

Exploring the Story is designed to help students see what is not necessarily explicit in the text and to note connections between different components of the story. Students are asked to use the textual evidence to support their answers. The questions are aimed at different learning styles.

Exploring the Vocabulary and **Exploring the Language** provide practice of important vocabulary from the story in a new context. They also describe different aspects of style and usage in English.

Exploring the Writing takes advantage of each unit's style to briefly introduce the student to several stylistic aspects of written English.

Exploring Your Ideas encourages students to respond freely to different aspects of the story using their personal knowledge of the world, their ideas, and their feelings. The topics can be used as springboards for discussions, in essays, as entries in a journal, or in email or chat room exchanges.

Exploring the Internet offers more opportunities for interfacing with English. We hope that students will explore different aspects of the country represented by the story, as well as the customs and ideas it addresses. We encourage them to explore on their own and share their discoveries with classmates and teachers. The sites were current at the time of publication and were screened with young adults in mind. They do not constitute any endorsement on our part of the ideas or products featured.

Follow-Up Activities provides a variety of challenges suited to different student populations. Students are not expected to complete all of these assignments. Rather, they should be encouraged to choose those exercises that appeal to their special interests and talents. The range of assignments presented in this section means that there is something for every ability level. The completed projects can provide contributions to a portfolio, i.e., a letter, composition, poem, photograph, drawing or painting, scene from a play, journal entry, research project, etc. Teachers should use their discretion as to how many and which of these activities are suitable for their students.

Exploring What You Read, the last section of the book, provides an opportunity to compare and contrast different aspects of the material the students have read, and to express their opinions on different topics and on the book as a whole. We are interested in the teachers' and students' feedback and will read your comments with great interest.

FB

Acknowledgements

We wish to thank Aaron Berman of Alta Books Center Publishers for his interest in and enthusiasm for this project. He has been a source of support and ideas. Alta's editor, Jamie Cross, was unfailingly kind and helpful whenever we called on her expertise, patiently explaining and clarifying as the need arose. Her assistant, Raissa Burns, also made meaningful contributions in getting the book to its final stage.

Some teachers took time out of their busy teaching schedules to test the material in its early stages. They are: Priscilla Butler, Wayne Hill, and Don Richardson. We thank them and their students for their valuable feedback.

Our greatest debt is to Sara Tanke, content editor extraordinaire. Her high standards of excellence were evident in her many pertinent remarks, corrections, and suggestions, most of which were incorporated in the final version of *Views and Voices*.

Every effort was made to obtain permission to reprint all the selections in this book. Credits below are given in the order in which the stories appear:

"Amina" by Shirley Saad from International Feminist Fiction. Previously printed in *Opening the Gates: A Century of Arab Feminist Writing*, edited by Margot Badran and Miriam Cooke. Copyright © Indiana University Press 1990. Reprinted by permission of Indiana University Press.

Excerpts from *Every Light in the House Burnin'* by Andrea Levy, published by Headline Book Publishing. Copyright © Andrea Levy 1994. Reprinted by permission of the author's agent, David Grossman Literary Agency Ltd.

"Family Album" by Siv Cedering from *Sudden Fiction International*. First published in The Georgia Review. Copyright © Siv Cedering 1978, 1989. Reprinted by permission of the author.

"The Visit" by Catherine Lim from *Or Else, The Lightening God and Other Stories* by Catherine Lim, published by Heinemann Asia, a division of Reed Elsevier (Singapore) Pte Ltd Consumer Education Books. Copyright © Catherine Lim 1980. Reprinted by permission of the author.

"Spring Love" chapter from *House of the Winds* by Mia Yun, published by Interlink Books, an imprint of Interlink Publishing Group, Inc. Copyright © Mia Yun 1998. Reprinted by permission of Interlink Publishing.

PART ONE

In the Family

I used to wonder what mark I had to prove I was born.
Siv Cedering, Family Album

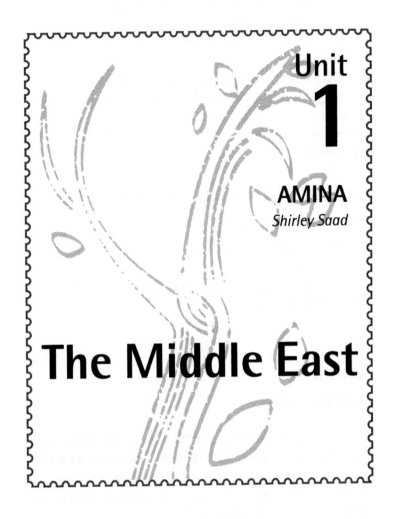

Unit
1

AMINA
Shirley Saad

The Middle East

Well, there would be no henna and celebration for this girl.

The Middle East

Unit
1

AMINA
Shirley Saad

INTRODUCTION

Think about and/or discuss these questions:

1. In many cultures, it has been traditional for a couple to want sons. What might some of the reasons be behind this preference? Are sons still preferred today? Discuss.
2. Is there a special ceremony or party after a baby is born in your country? Who participates? What happens? Are there different ceremonies for boys and girls?
3. How many children do you think make a "perfect-sized" family? Explain why.
4. In your country, are babies generally born at home or in a hospital?
5. In your culture, what are some of the reasons a man might divorce his wife or a wife divorce her husband?
6. In your country, are men and women allowed to work together? Live in the same space? Eat together? Touch?

LIBRARY/INTERNET TASKS

Before you read the story:

1. Find a world map that shows countries where Islam is the main religion.
2. Find information about how Muslim men and women dress in different Islamic countries.

Amina

Shirley Saad

Shirley Saad was born in Egypt to a Polish-Romanian mother and a Lebanese father. She was educated by Irish nuns. She has always felt torn between her European heritage and education, and her Arab origins and environment. She has written many short stories about the lives of women in the Arab world.

The bold words should be learned. The numbered words are explained to help you understand the story. Some words have more than one meaning. The meaning we give is the closest synonym.

Amina opened her eyes and for a moment wondered where she was. Then she remembered and a **moan** escaped her lips. The English nurse hurried over and bent down, "Don't you worry now," she said. "You'll be fine and the baby is all right."

Amina asked, **not daring** to hope, "Is it a boy or a girl?"

"A girl," replied the nurse cheerfully. "A beautiful, bouncing[1], four kilograms girl. *Mabruk*, congratulations."

"*Allah yi barek fi omrek*[2]," murmured Amina as she **sank back** on her pillows. Another girl!

What a **catastrophe**. What would happen to her now? She had brought four girls into the world, four girls in six years of marriage. She felt tears running down her cheeks, and she remembered how proud and happy she had been when her mother had told her she was engaged to be married.

She had seen Hamid twice, once at her cousin's house when he arrived **unexpectedly**. The girls all scattered[3] to their quarters to put on their **masks and veils**. The next time, he came with his father to ask for her hand in marriage. The houseboy serving the coffee told the Indian housegirl who in turn ran and told her mistress. So, she had gone to peek through[4] the partition[5] between the men's and women's *majilis*[6]. She saw Hamid and his father sipping[7] coffee and being congratulated by all the men in the family. They **embraced** and rubbed noses, big smiles on everyone's faces.

☞ Why does Amina cry after the birth of her baby?
☞ When does she see her husband before they are married?
☞ What do the girls do when Hamid arrives at her house?

Amina remembered her wedding, the noise and the bustle[8], her hennaed[9] hands and feet, the whispers among the older women which frightened her and the **anticipation**. Finally, she found herself alone with this stranger, who had turned out to be[10] very kind and gentle and **considerate**.

Well, there would be no henna and celebration for this girl. God, why couldn't she have a boy? Just one, that's all she wanted, just one little baby boy. She wished the **midwife** hadn't told her when she **had the miscarriage** that it had been a boy. The only one in six years and she had to go and lose it. It was her fault too. She had no business climbing a ladder at five months. She slipped and fell and the doctors kept her in the hospital for a week, then told her she was all right and could go home. But there was no movement, no life, so she went back to the hospital and after two weeks of tests and X-rays and hope and **despair**, they finally decided the baby was dead.

Left margin notes:

1 bouncing: very active

2 *Allah yi barek fi omrek* (Arabic): May God send blessings to your life

3 scattered: ran in different directions

4 peek through: take a quick look

5 partition: division in a room

6 *majilis* (Arabic): areas where men and women sit separately

7 sipping: drinking in small quantities

8 bustle: running around

9 hennaed: painted with reddish-brown dye

10 turned out to be: to show a different side than what was expected

---

Right margin glossary:

moan: long, low, sad sound *(make sound)*

not daring: afraid

sank back: laid back, reclined *(body language)*

catastrophe: terrible thing, disaster

unexpectedly: as a surprise

masks and veils: cloth coverings for the face and head *(show pic)*

embraced: *(hug)* put their arms around each other

anticipation: excitement about what is coming

considerate: thoughtful of others *(sentence / context)*

midwife: woman who helps at childbirth

had the miscarriage: had the baby too early

despair: deep unhappiness

After that she had two more girls, and now the fourth.

Would Hamid divorce her? Would he take a second wife? His older brother had been pressing for[11] two years, urging[12] him to take a second wife. Hamid loved Amina and his daughters, but he was human. He did have all that money and the social and political position and no boy to leave it to.

Her mother came in, then her sisters-in-law. Each one kissed her and said, "*Mabruk*[13]," but she could tell they were not really happy. Her mother was especially fearful for her daughter's future and felt that some of the **disgrace** fell on her and the family too. The sisters-in-law were secretly jubilant[14], because they had boys. Hamid's social **status** and half his fortune would revert to[15] their own sons if he never had boys of his own. Of course, he was still young and he and Amina might try again. But for the moment the in-laws felt **reassured** and falsely commiserated[16] with Amina on her bad luck.

"It's God's will," they murmured, smiling under their masks. Their mouths were sad but Amina could see the **twinkle** in their eyes. "God's will be done."

☞ What happens to Amina in her second pregnancy?
☞ What advice does Hamid receive from his older brother?
☞ What is Amina's mother afraid of?
☞ What do Amina's sisters-in-law hope?

Friends started coming into the room. They kissed Amina and said, "*Mabruk*," then sat on the floor, cross-legged. Arranging their robes around them, they sipped coffee from little thimble cups[17], eating fruits and sweets.

Her cousin Huda came too. She wore a long, velvet dress, embroidered[18] on the sides and bodice[19], loose and flowing, to conceal her **belly**. She was in the sixth month and looked radiantly serene[20].

Amina thought **bitterly**, "She already has two daughters and three sons. What does she need another baby for? She's not so young anymore."

As if she read her thoughts, Huda said, "This is my last baby. It will be a baby for my old age. The others are married or away at school all day. An empty house is a sad house. You need many sons and daughters to keep your husband happy. You are still young, Amina. God has given you four daughters, maybe the next four will be boys, God's will be done."

"As God wills it, so be it," **murmured** the other ladies smugly[21].

---

disgrace: social failure, disapproval

status: position, rank

reassured: free from anxiety

twinkle: small, bright light

belly: stomach

bitterly: with anger and sadness

murmured: whispered

---

11 pressing for: speaking urgently

12 urging: insisting

13 *mabruk* (Arabic): congratulations

14 jubilant: very happy

15 revert to: return to

16 commiserated: sympathized

17 thimble cups: very small cups

18 embroidered: decorated with stitched designs

19 bodice: top part of a dress

20 radiantly serene: shining with peaceful happiness

21 smugly: with self-satisfaction

22 deferentially:
   with polite respect

23 repudiated:
   rejected, divorced

24 burst into:
   suddenly began

25 crows:
   large, noisy, black birds

26 eager for: excited for

27 solicitously:
   with love and concern

28 year's reprieve:
   a year of delay,
   temporary relief

Hamid came in and the ladies all stood up deferentially[22], and **hastily** went into the next room. The maid served them more coffee. Hamid looked at his wife, tried to smile and searched for something nice to say. He thought she must be tired, disappointed, ashamed of having failed him one more time and afraid of being repudiated[23].

He sat down near the bed and said, "Well, mother of my children, we will just have to try again, won't we?"

Amina burst into[24] tears of sorrow, shame, and relief.

"Don't cry," he said, **distressed**. "The important thing is that you and the girls are in good health," he said smiling. "As long as we are young we will try again, eh?"

Amina **blushed** under her mask and pulled her veil around her face. He patted her hand, got up, and left the room.

The ladies came rushing back in, like a flock of crows[25], eager for[26] the news, good or bad.

Amina's mother said solicitously[27], "What did he say, my daughter?" He said better luck next time, Mother!"

The mother let out a sigh of relief. They had another year's reprieve[28]. The women congratulated Amina and left to spread the news.

Amina sank back on her pillows and **drifted off to sleep.**

hastily: quickly

distressed: upset

blushed: turned red

drifted off to sleep:
slowly went to sleep

⟨ Why is Amina's cousin Huda having another baby?
⟨ Why does Amina start crying?
⟨ What is most important to Hamid?
⟨ What is Hamid's solution?

EXPLORING THE STORY

AN ACTIVITY FOR GROUP DISCUSSION, HOMEWORK, OR YOUR JOURNAL

A good writer will not only describe interesting characters and an interesting plot—what happens in the story—but will also provide extra ideas or opinions that are not always easy to see.

Read the questions below and think about them. Always go back to the story to explain your answers.

1. Why do you think the author begins the story with the contrast of the cheerful English nurse and Amina's tears? *Contrast between Western & Middle Eastern point of view.*

2. Why does Amina accept the blame for having only daughters?

3. Consider the other characters in the story. Who gives Amina support? *Her husband, Huda* Who does not and why? Who is her best ally (supporter)? *Her sister-in-law* *Her husband*

4. Choose five adjectives that describe Hamid. Explain your choices. *gentle, considerate, caring, loving, respectful,*

EXPLORING THE VOCABULARY

Complete the following sentences with bold words from the story.
Change the form of the word when necessary.

1. In some countries, a man and woman cannot _embrace_
   in the street.
2. I felt such _despair_ ~~distressed~~ when I failed my driving
   test again.
3. The girl _blushed_ when he told others how much
   he loved her.
4. They could see the _twinkling_ of candles in the window.
5. In a hospital ward, patients sometimes _moaned_
   in pain.
6. An earthquake can be a _catastrophe_ for highly
   populated areas.
7. In some countries, copying your friend's answers at school is a
   disgrace .
8. He _murmured_ an excuse to the teacher as he arrived
   late to class.
9. When Susan heard the sad news, she was _distressed_ .

Now choose ten of the numbered words and write a sentence for
each one. You may copy sentences from your dictionary.

EXPLORING THE LANGUAGE

LANGUAGE CHUNKS

Many students like to learn fixed expressions (words that usually go
together) and then use these "chunks" of language in speaking or writing.
This kind of learning is very common when you learn your first language.
We recommend that you learn these language chunks.

Here is a list of chunks from "Amina." Study them. They are explained
in the margins of the story.

sank back	turned out to be
peek through	burst into
pressing for	revert to
year's reprieve	eager for
drifted off	

Now complete these sentences with one of the expressions, changing the form of the words when necessary.

1. Everyone was __eager for__ the dance contest to begin.
2. Of all the participants, most of the crowd was __pressing for__ the couple wearing green shirts to win.
3. At the sound of the music, the dancers __bursted into__ action. They danced as if they were on fire!
4. Who would win? As good as the couple wearing green looked, everyone's attention kept __peeking through__ ~~reverting~~ the dancers in purple.
5. Unexpectedly, the judges took hours to decide. It __turned out to be__ the longest dance contest in history!

EXPLORING THE WRITING

ITALICS

Italics are used in a text for different reasons:

1. To indicate the title of a book, movie, song, or newspaper.
   The title of this book is *Views and Voices*.
2. To indicate the name of a ship, car, plane or any other vehicle.
   He sailed to England on *The Empire Windrush*.
3. To put an emphasis on a word or group of words. In this unit, the directions for the exercises are italicized (written in italics).
4. To identify foreign words and phrases.
   "*Mabruk*, congratulations."

Note that frequently the author will directly give you the meaning of the word, as in example 4. If not, you can often guess the meaning of a word or a phrase by its context (the information in the sentences around the italicized word). Of course, you should always look for clues in the text when you come across an English word that you don't know.

Look rapidly through the texts of Unit 5 and Unit 9. Write down the italicized words and check which of the above four categories they belong to.

EXPLORING YOUR IDEAS

AN ACTIVITY FOR GROUP DISCUSSION, HOMEWORK, OR YOUR JOURNAL

Read these sentences from the story and respond with your ideas and feelings. Discuss or write as much as possible because, as you do, more ideas will come to you.

1. Well, there would be no henna and celebration for this girl.
2. Hamid loved Amina and his daughters, but he was only human.
3. Hamid came in and all the ladies stood up deferentially and hastily went into the next room.
4. The ladies came back in, like a flock of crows, eager for the news, good or bad.
5. They had another year's reprieve.

EXPLORING THE INTERNET

Learn more about women's lives in the Arab world at **www.al-bab.com/arab/women.htm**. You'll find articles on the history of women in the Middle East and on present-day issues from marriage to childbirth.

Connect with women's issues at **www.aviva.org**, a free women's Web magazine. See the magazine's section, **www.aviva.org/mideast.htm**, for news specific to women in the Middle East.

What can you do to help improve the lives of women in the Middle East? There are several organizations committed to helping and supporting Muslim women. See **www.mwlusa.org** (a nonprofit American Muslim organization working towards women's rights) and **www.womenforwomen.org/index.htm** (a program that connects women in the United States with female survivors of political, social, and economic oppression in countries across the world).

At **www.kamilat.org**, you'll find surprising, believe-it-or-not global statistics on women and girls (click on the "International Statistics on Women" link at the bottom of the home page).

How is Arabic written and pronounced? You can see and hear the language (and take an online course!) at **lexicorient.com/babel/arabic/index.htm**.

We encourage you to do your own Internet search and share the sites you find with your classmates and with your teacher.

FOLLOW-UP ACTIVITIES

Choose one or more of the following activities to complete:

1. Do research to find out which parent determines the sex of a baby. Make a presentation or write a paragraph about it.
2. Is it better to be the eldest or the youngest child in your family? Interview your classmates and report their opinions to the class.
3. Write a conversation between Hamid and his older brother on the topic of taking a second wife. Act out the scene in front of the class.
4. Compare the marriage customs of your culture and another culture. What is similar? What is different?
5. Imagine that you are Amina's mother. Write a letter to your best friend to tell her your thoughts and feelings about the birth of your granddaughter.
6. Amina will have no celebration for her baby. What do you think this little girl's life will be like in the future?
7. If you are a parent, write about the birth of your child. If you are not, imagine you are Hamid and write a journal entry on the birth of your new daughter and your feelings toward your wife.
8. Write a different ending to the story beginning when Hamid walks into Amina's room after she has given birth to another baby girl.

If you enjoyed reading "Amina," we suggest that you read the other short stories in the anthologies, *International Feminist Fiction* and *Opening the Gates: A Century of Arab Feminist Writing*. See the acknowledgements page for publishing information.

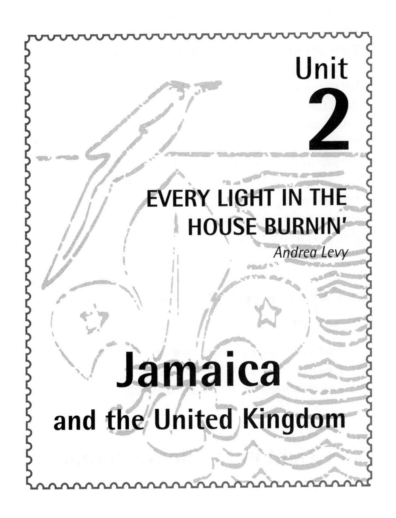

Unit 2

EVERY LIGHT IN THE HOUSE BURNIN'

Andrea Levy

Jamaica
and the United Kingdom

My dad called my mum 'Mum' and my mum called my dad 'Dad'.
I was about ten years old before I knew their actual names—Winston and Beryl.

Unit 2

EVERY LIGHT IN THE
HOUSE BURNIN'
Andrea Levy

Jamaica
and the United Kingdom

INTRODUCTION

Think about and/or discuss these questions:

1. In what ways are your parents different from or similar to your grandparents?
2. In what ways are your parents similar to each other? How are they different? How are you different from or similar to your parents?
3. As a child, what did you know about your father's or mother's jobs? Explain.
4. If you are a parent, how much does your child know about your life outside the home?
5. Is it easy or difficult for you to ask your parents personal questions? Give an example of a personal question you would ask your parents and one you wouldn't ask.
6. What kind of activities do your parents enjoy in their leisure time?
7. Did your parents have similar educations? Explain.
8. Do you know anyone who continued to study after marriage? Give examples.
9. Did you or your parents emigrate from another country? If so, what were the reasons for emigration? What was difficult in the new country?

LIBRARY/INTERNET TASKS

Before you read the story:

1. Find out information on Jamaica: location, people, and history.
2. Find out how many people of Jamaican descent live in Britain.
3. Find a description of the British Open University.

Every Light in the House Burnin'
Andrea Levy

Andrea Levy's family comes from Jamaica. She was born in London in 1956. Following are two excerpts (short sections) from her first novel *Every Light in the House Burnin'.* She has written three novels and was one of the first successful black writers in Britain.

The bold words should be learned. The numbered words are explained to help you understand the story. Some words have more than one meaning. The meaning we give is the closest synonym.

EXCERPT 1: MY DAD

My dad was a man—most dads are. But my dad had been taught or was shown or **picked up** that a man was certain things and a woman was others. I don't know whether he ever questioned the assumptions[1] but I can identify him now as a man **thought up** in the 1930s and 40s.

He was head of a family—a breadwinner[2]. He should go out to work in the morning and come home at night. He had to **discipline** children and **occasionally** do things around the home that required some degree of physical strength. A man did not have to be loving and **affectionate**. A man had to know everything and never be seen not to understand the world. A man would help around the house only when asked but a man always emptied the bins[3].

My dad was a man and he did what he thought was expected of him. But he couldn't understand when more was **demanded**.

'What!' He'd say if he had to take any of us to the dentist. 'What!' if expected to **wash up**. And 'Oh my God!' if my mum ever announced that she would not be in so he'd have to look after us.

My dad was from Jamaica—born and bred[4]. He came to this country in 1948 on the *Empire Windrush*[5] ship. My mum joined him six months later in his one room in Earl's Court. He never talked about his family or his life in Jamaica. He seemed only to **exist** in one plane[6] of time—the present. There is an old photo of him—grainy[7] black and white that shows him dressed in an immaculate[8] tailored[9] suit with wide baggy[10] trousers, wearing a shirt with a collar held by a pin, and a **proper** tie. His hair is short and well groomed[11]. He is standing by a chair in the grounds of what looks to be a beautiful house. The photo looks like my dad as a 'Great Gatsby'[12]-type millionaire. When I asked my dad about the photo that **fascinated** me, he would grudgingly admit[13] that it was where he lived. But when I pressed[14] him to tell me more he would shrug[15] and tell me not to bother him. Or he'd suck his teeth and ask me why I was interested. He would ask this in the manner of somebody who does not want an answer—of somebody who would like you to leave them alone.

My dad had a job with the Post Office. He'd been in the same job for as long as I knew him. I'm afraid I can't tell you if he enjoyed his work—if he longed to go every day because it brought him fulfillment[16] and happiness—or whether he dreaded[17] every morning and **watched the clock** until he could leave. I can't tell you because I don't know. My dad was a man and men didn't talk about their work. It was a secret between him and his **wage packet**. If you asked him what he did at work, he'd shrug and say he worked for the Post Office.

---

1 assumptions: beliefs

2 breadwinner: person who earns the family money

3 bins (British): trash or rubbish cans

4 born and bred: born and educated

5 Empire Windrush: a famous ship that transported immigrants

6 plane: level

7 grainy: rough, unclear

8 immaculate: perfectly clean

9 tailored: made to order

10 baggy: loose

11 well-groomed: neat

12 *Great Gatsby*: book about elegant millionaires in the 1920s

13 grudgingly admit: state or say unwillingly

14 pressed: pushed

15 shrug: move his shoulders up and down

16 fulfillment: satisfaction

17 dreaded: feared

---

picked up: learned

thought up: developing

discipline: control, punish

occasionally: sometimes

affectionate: loving

demanded: required

wash up: wash the dishes

exist: live

proper: good

fascinated: interested

watched the clock: wanted to leave

wage packet: salary, income

My dad called my mum 'Mum' and my mum called my dad 'Dad'. I was about ten years old before I knew their **actual** names—Winston and Beryl. My dad didn't like anyone to know his name. It was another secret. If we said it in public he would look **embarrassed** and tell us not to say it again. And if we said it too loudly at home he would tell us to be quiet. As for my dad's age—well that was shrug-shoulders age, that was **absolutely**-none-of-my-business age, that was don't-bother-me age.

☆ When and where was the father born?
☆ How does the father see his role in the family?
☆ How much do his children know about his past? Why?
☆ What kind of work does he do at the post office?
☆ What were some of the things he would not discuss with his children?

I should describe my dad—tell you what he looked like. But who would I describe? Should I describe the young man I knew with neatly greased-back[18] **wavy** hair, who would throw me up in the air or ask to hold my hand when we crossed the road.

Or should I tell you about the pot-bellied[19] middle-aged man who spent hours in front of the mirror trying to **conceal** his grey hair. Or perhaps I should describe the old, wild-haired[20] man—fat and bloated[21] by steroids[22] **aimed at keeping** his dying body alive a little longer. My dad was all these men and many more. Some said he showed a resemblance[23] to the late President Sadat of Egypt in his younger days. And he did sometimes—around the nose.

My dad was on the **late shift** at the Post Office—he started work at twelve noon and finished at eight o'clock at night. This shift meant, **by accident** or design[24], that he managed to **avoid** any prolonged[25] **contact** with his family. He was never an **early riser** and would spend the frantic[26] morning rush propped up[27] in bed with a cigarette, the Daily Mirror[28] and breakfast on a tray. He didn't get up until everyone was safely out.

In the school holidays I would sit with him during his two hours and watch his **routine**. He got up and made every bed in the flat[29], with the **blank** expression of a job **performed** but not remembered. He **tugged at** sheets, flattened blankets, plumped[30] pillows until every bed was neat, ready for another night's sleep.

After this he'd neaten[31] himself. He dressed in a suit every day. He didn't have many suits but the ones he did have were all the same. They all had wide baggy trousers with turn-ups[32] at the bottom. They were all in shades of grey and only my dad could tell the difference between them.

actual: real

embarrassed: uncomfortable, ashamed

absolutely: completely

wavy: not straight

conceal: hide

aimed at keeping: trying to keep

late shift: late working hours

by accident: not on purpose

avoid: keep away from

contact: communication, interaction

early riser: one who gets up early

routine: usual, regular actions

blank: empty

performed: done

tugged at: pulled

18 greased-back: flat, combed

19 pot-bellied: with a fat stomach

20 wild-haired: with hair not brushed

21 bloated: swollen, fat

22 steroids: medicine

23 resemblance: similarity

24 by design: on purpose

25 prolonged: long, lasting

26 frantic: very busy

27 propped up: sitting with a pillow behind the back

28 Daily Mirror: British newspaper

29 flat (British): apartment

30 plumped: made bigger and softer by shaking

31 neaten: make tidy

32 turn-ups: cuffs

33 dabbed: put on

34 buffed:
    made shiny, polished

35 Brylcreem:
    brand of hair oil

36 stroked: brushed

37 glaze: bright finish

38 lapels:
    folds on the front
    collar of a coat

39 pigeon-like: bird-like

40 bobbing: nodding

41 shrunk her down:
    made her smaller

42 privileged treatment:
    better service

43 council:
    people in charge
    of the town

44 council estate:
    public housing

45 coal:
    black mineral
    burned for heat

When he was dressed, my dad sat on the edge of the bed and polished his shoes. He dabbed[33] some polish on the brush, then rubbed it **furiously** into the leather with a motion that shook his body and the bed. Then he buffed[34] them until they shone.

furiously: very hard

He brushed his hair in the same way. Using a different brush and **substituting** polish **for** Brylcreem[35], he stroked[36] every hair into place until he had a shiny black glaze[37] on his head.

substituting for: using in place of

He would always wear a tie which he would **knot** without looking. Then lastly he'd put on his jacket and adjust the lapels[38] with a strange pigeon-like[39] movement of the neck, bobbing[40] his head and straightening the **fabric** at the same time.

knot: tie

fabric: cloth

☆ Why does the speaker have a problem describing her father?
☆ What happened to him as he got older?
☆ Why didn't he see much of his family?
☆ What did the father do every morning after he woke up?
☆ How did he prepare himself for work?

EXCERPT 2: MY MUM

My mum was a teacher—a teacher of young children. She began her working career in Jamaica where she earned her own living. Then she married my dad and they decided to come to England to find 'better opportunity.'

My mum was a tall woman, taller than my dad but the years shrunk her down[41]. She had a head of thick black hair, which waved and curled any way she pleased. My mum's nose was large and wide and her lips thick. But her skin was pale. In Jamaica, they sometimes wouldn't serve her in shops, thinking that she was white, or sometimes she'd get privileged treatment[42] for exactly the same reason.

My mum joined my dad in his one room in London. But the English wouldn't let her teach. They said she had to retrain before she could stand before English children. My mum didn't have the money to retrain and then she **became pregnant**, so she **took in** sewing at home instead.

became pregnant: expected a child

My mum had four children. Three within one year of each other—two girls, Yvonne and Patricia, then a boy, John. Four years later she had me, Angela. The council[43] gave my mum and dad a flat—a **temporary** flat on an old thirties' red brick council estate[44]. They said it was just until they found something more **suitable**, but that was before I was born and I lived there until I was twenty-one.

took in: accepted

temporary: short-term

suitable: fit, appropriate

She looked after her four children and one husband in the small three-bedroom flat. There was no garden and the only sources of heat were coal[45] and electric fires.

warmed up: became warm

permanently: forever

My mum was always cold, she never **warmed up**. 'This country is coooold', she would say. She'd sit so near the fire that her legs became **permanently** red and blotchy[46]. And she never took her coat off—she would cook or wash or sit, all in her outside coat.

'Aren't you taking your coat off, Mum?'

'I will—when I warm up,' she'd say. She made all her four children wear layers and layers of clothes[47] because she was 'coooold'.

☆ Why do the parents leave Jamaica?
☆ How is the mother treated in Jamaica? Why?
☆ Why does the mother have to take in sewing in England?
☆ Why is the mother cold all the time?

When I was five and old enough to go to school, my mum decided she'd had enough of sewing and went back to college to become again what she'd always been—a teacher. After three years of washing, cooking, college, feeding, homework, bed, washing, cooking, college, feeding, homework, bed, she got her **diploma**.

diploma: certificate, degree

My mum was an educated woman and she wanted to do what educated people did. Listen to classical music[48], but we only played soul[49], Tamla Motown and pop—'It's got no words, Mum, and no **beat**'. Have stimulating[50] conversation—'Shut up, Mum. I can't hear the **telly**'. Go to the theatre—'What you wanna go out for, you can see everything you want on the television and it's free'. And to talk **properly**—'Do what, Mum? Leave it out. I **ain't talkin'** like that'!'

beat: rhythm
telly (British slang): television

properly: correctly

ain't talkin' (slang): am not talking

So my mum took an Open University degree in Humanities[51] and Social Science[52]. She watched the programmes in the early mornings then went to work to teach 'her' children. At night she went to the shops and bought food, then carried it home, in two carrier bags, 'to balance meself up'. She made her family their evening meal, then went into her bedroom to study. The room was too small to hold a desk and chair. My mum sat on the edge of the bed and splayed[53] her books out around her and read and wrote for her degree. In the summer she went to summer schools at universities and would come back with tales[54] of nice food she ate, the lovely rooms she studied in and the educated people she met. After several years she got a BA[55].

passport: document for travel

My mum then wanted to visit her relations in America and Jamaica. She needed a **passport**. They wouldn't let her have one. After thirty-eight years of living in Britain, teaching British children, paying British taxes, learning British ways, she wasn't British. She needed to apply and pay 200 **pounds**.

pounds: English money

46 blotchy: discolored

47 layers of clothes: clothes on top of clothes

48 classical music: music of great composers of the past

49 soul: emotional black music

50 stimulating: exciting

51 Humanities: study of literature, art, philosophy, etc.

52 Social Science: study of history, sociology, etc.

53 splayed: spread

54 tales: stories

55 BA: university degree (Bachelor of Arts)

☆ When and why does the mother stop sewing?

☆ Describe a typical day's work for the mother.

☆ Give three examples to show how the mother and the rest of her family have different tastes. Where and what does the mother study?

☆ Is the mother successful with her studies?

☆ Why does she want a passport?

EXPLORING THE STORY

AN ACTIVITY FOR GROUP DISCUSSION, HOMEWORK, OR YOUR JOURNAL

A good writer will not only describe interesting characters and an interesting plot—what happens in the story—but will also provide extra ideas or opinions that are not always easy to see.

Answer the activities and questions below. Always go back to the story to explain your answers.

1. The narrator gives us a child's view of her parents, two people who have very different personalities as well as some common ideas. By using the words "Dad" and "Mum," the narrator uses the point of view of a child looking at her parents. She tells us about what children look for in a parent, what they need, and what they appreciate. Look at the words in the list below. Decide which describe the mom (M), which describe the dad (D) and which describe both (B) or neither (N). Discuss your answers with other students.

___ ambition   ___ persevere

___ secret   ___ mysterious

___ emigrate   ___ nervous

___ funny   ___ affection

___ hard worker   ___ responsibility

___ responsible   ___ discipline

___ lonely   ___ absent

___ jealous   ___ education

___ cold   ___ improve

___ interesting   ___ graduate

___ neatness

Now use these words to write a paragraph about Angela's parents. The paragraph should describe how her parents are alike and how they are different.

2. The characters in this story want different things from each other. What does the father want? What does the mother want? What does the narrator (Angela) want? Do they get what they want from each other? Explain.

3. If Angela becomes a parent, what lessons will she have learned from her childhood?

4. In what ways did the race of Angela's parents influence their lives? Make a list.

EXPLORING THE VOCABULARY

Complete the following sentences with bold words from the story. Change the form of the word when necessary.

1. My father was a very strict man. He believed in _disciplining_ us.

2. Sometimes he could be _affectionate_ and loving.

3. He always expected _proper_ behavior from his children.

4. He _demanded_ obedience from us at all times.

5. He became _embarrassed_ and upset when we didn't take him seriously.

6. My mother also expected us to behave _properly_.

7. She didn't like us to use slang. When we said _ain't_, she made us say "am not."

8. Sometimes we objected to this _demand furiously_

9. We had to speak correctly during our _content_ at the dinner table.

10. She made sure that we only watched _suitable_ programs on television.

Now choose ten of the numbered words and write a sentence for each one. You may copy sentences from your dictionary.

EXPLORING THE LANGUAGE

LANGUAGE CHUNKS

Many students like to learn fixed expressions (words that usually go together) and then use these "chunks" of language in speaking or writing. This kind of learning is very common when you learn your first language. We recommend that you learn these language chunks.

Here is a list of chunks from the story excerpts. Study them. They are explained in the margins of the story.

picked up	wash up
watch the clock	born and bred
aimed at	late shift
early riser	propped up
took in	warmed up

Now complete these sentences with one of the above expressions, changing the form of the words when necessary.

1. It's really easy to _____ warm up _____ food in a microwave oven.
2. In the old days, some new immigrants _____ took in _____ washing and ironing to make money.
3. Would you please _____ pick up _____ the children after school?
4. My father was a gentlemen, _____ born and bred _____.
5. After eating your dinner, _____ wash up _____ the dishes and put them away.
6. My new job is good except that I have to work the _____ late shift _____.
7. As you know, I'm not an _____ early riser _____, and it will not be easy to get up in the morning.
8. When I went to see Alice in the hospital, she was sitting _____ propped up _____ in bed.
9. The robber picked up his gun and _____ aimed at _____ the detective.
10. If you love your work, you probably don't _____ watch the clock _____.

EXPLORING THE WRITING

BRITISH AND AMERICAN ENGLISH

How you learn to spell depends on whether your teachers teach British English or American English. The differences are not great and you will soon become used to them. Below is a list of common words that vary in spelling:

BRITISH	AMERICAN
centre	center
cheque	check
colour	color
criticise	criticize
grey	gray
labour	labor
odour	odor
organise	organize
programme	program
theatre	theater

This is not a complete list but it will give you an idea of the variations you can expect. In the same way there are variations in spelling, there are variations in vocabulary. Here are some of the differences in vocabulary between British and American English:

BRITISH	AMERICAN
autumn	fall
bill (restaurant)	check
biscuit	cookie
flat	apartment
chemist	drugstore
the cinema	the movies
cross	mad
cupboard	closet
dustbin	garbage can, trash can
estate agent	realtor
film	movie
garden	backyard
ground floor	first floor
ill	sick
lift	elevator
mad	crazy

mobile (phone)	cellular
nasty	mean
nursery	preschool
pram	buggy
post	mail
postcode	zip code
public toilet	restroom
queue (wait)	line up
return (ticket)	round-trip
rubbish	garbage, trash
rubbish-bin	garbage can, trash can
shop	store
single (ticket)	one-way
telly	TV
timetable	schedule
underground (train)	subway
waistcoat	vest
zip	zipper
diary	calendar

In this textbook, some of the stories are written in British English and others in American English. In the vocabulary definitions, *(British)* identifies British usage and the American equivalent is given. In the exercises we use American English.

The most important thing to know is that both forms of English are correct. The one you use will depend on where you are studying English, which English your instructor is teaching, and with whom you want to communicate. Your goal should be to understand either one without difficulty.

EXPLORING YOUR IDEAS

AN ACTIVITY FOR GROUP DISCUSSION, HOMEWORK, OR YOUR JOURNAL

Read these sentences from the story and respond with your ideas and feelings. Discuss or write as much as possible because, as you do, more ideas will come to you.

1. But the English wouldn't let her teach...
2. But he couldn't understand when more was demanded.
3. My mum was an educated woman and she wanted to do what educated people do.
4. It was another secret.

5. ...then went to work to teach "her" children.
6. This shift meant, by accident or by design, that he managed to avoid any prolonged contact with his family.

EXPLORING THE INTERNET

Would you like to know more about Jamaica?
Go to **www.jamaicans.com**, a site filled with information on Jamaica today—culture, people, and music.

At **www.bbc.co.uk/arts/books/windrush**, you'll feel as if you were aboard the famous *Empire Windrush,* the ship that carried 492 Jamaican immigrants to Britain in 1948. Its voyage represents a very important moment in the history of Black Britain.

Do you know that, as a child, Andrea Levy was embarrassed that her parents were not English? Read her article on identity and life in a multicultural society at **elt.britcoun.org.pl/i_engl.htm**.

Visit post office sites around the world, including the BPO (British Post Office), at **www.postoffice.com**.

The Open University is Britain's largest university, with over 200,000 students. At **www.open.ac.uk** and **www.open2.net**, you can check what courses the university offers.

We encourage you to do your own Internet search and share the sites you find with your classmates and with your teacher.

FOLLOW-UP ACTIVITIES

Choose one or more of the following activities to complete:

1. Describe the personality and habits of your father, mother, or any other person who raised you. Write a composition describing this person.
2. Take a photograph, paint, or draw a picture of your family. Share it with your classmates.
3. Compose a song or poem about a member of your family.
4. What names do you call your mother and father? Have you used different names at different times in your life? Ask four or five people these questions and write a paragraph about your findings.
5. The narrator's father developed his ideas about being a man in the 1930s and 1940s. How are the men you know similar to and different from him? Write a short composition about your comparisons.

6. Interview some people who have lived in two very different climates. Write a few paragraphs about their experiences.

7. Write a dialogue between a husband and wife who are planning to move to a new country. Discuss the positive and negative expectations of the move. You might enjoy doing this with a classmate.

If you enjoyed reading these excerpts from Andrea Levy's novel, we suggest that you read the whole book *Every Light in the House Burnin.'* See the acknowledgements page for publishing information.

FAMILY ALBUM

Siv Cedering

Sweden

I used to wonder what mark I had to prove I was born.

Unit
3

FAMILY ALBUM
Siv Cedering

Sweden

INTRODUCTION

Think about and/or discuss these questions:

1. How much do you know about your parents and grandparents? What pictures do you have of them? What stories do you know about them?
2. If you didn't know them, how do you imagine them?
3. How many names do you have? Who chose your names? What do most people call you?
4. In your culture, what are special things that families do after someone dies?
5. Has anyone in your family married a foreigner? How did they meet? What was the family's response?
6. What special talent do you have?
7. What does the word "communist" mean to you?
8. Do you think that some parts of your ancestors live on in you or do you believe you are a completely new and unique person?

LIBRARY/INTERNET TASKS

Before you read the story:

1. Find the locations of Sweden and Lapland.
2. Find out where Swedes have immigrated to in the past 100 years.
3. Find information on the origin of communism.

Family Album
Siv Cedering

Siv Cedering was born in Sweden and moved to the United States when she was a teenager. The author of eighteen books, she is bilingual and writes fiction and poetry in both English and Swedish.

The bold words should be learned. The numbered words are explained to help you understand the story. Some words have more than one meaning. The meaning we give is the closest synonym.

This is their wedding picture. Pappa wears a tuxedo[1], and Mamma is wearing a white satin[2] dress. She is smiling at the white lilies[3]. This is the house Pappa built for Mamma, when they were engaged. Then this house, then that; they were always making **blueprints** together.

blueprints:
plans for a new house

1 tuxedo: formal black suit

2 satin:
soft shiny material

3 lilies:
scented flowers

Mamma came from Lapland. She was quite poor and dreamed of pretty dresses. Her mother died when Mamma was small. Pappa met her when he came to Lapland as a conscientious objector[4]. He **preached** in her church. There he is with his **banjo**.

Pappa was quite poor too; everyone was in those days. He told me he didn't have any shoes that fit him, one spring, and he had to wear his father's big shoes. Pappa said he was so ashamed that he walked in the **ditch** all the way to school.

Pappa was one of eleven children, but only five of them grew up. The others died of **tuberculosis** or **diphtheria**. Three died in a six-week period, and Pappa says that death was accepted then, just like changes in the weather and a bad **crop** of potatoes. His parents were religious. I remember grandfather Anton rocking in the rocker[5] and riding on the reaper[6], and I remember Grandmother Maria, though I was just two when she died. The funeral was like a party: birch saplings[7] decorated the yard, relatives came from all around, and my sister and I wore new white dresses. Listen to the names of her eleven children:

Anna Viktoria, Karl Sigurd, Johan Martin, Hulda Maria, Signe Sofia, Bror Hilding, Judit Friedeborg, Brynhilt Elizabet, John Rudolf, Tore Adils, and Clary Torborg.

We called the eldest Tora. She was fat and never got married. Tore was the youngest son. I remember sitting next to him, eating blood pancakes[8] after a slaughter[9]. And calf-dance—a dish made from the first milk a cow gives after it has calved[10]. Tore recently left his wife and took a new one. He once told me that when he was a boy, he used to ski out in the dark afternoons of the North and stand still, watching the sky and feeling himself get smaller and smaller. This is Uncle Rudolf in his uniform, and this is Torborg, Pappa's youngest sister. Her fiancé had tried to make love to her once before they were married, and—Mamma told me—Torborg **tore** the engagement ring off her finger, threw it on the floor of the large farmhouse kitchen, and hollered[11], loud enough for everyone to hear: "What does that whoremonger[12] think I am?" He was the son of a big-city **mayor** and well educated, but **you can bet** he married a **virgin**. Don't they look good in this picture? Three of their five children are doctors. They say that Torborg got her temper from Great-grandfather. When he got drunk he cussed[13] and brought the horse into the kitchen. This is the Kell people from Kell farm. I am told I have the Kell eyes. Everyone on this side of the family hears ghosts and dreams **prophecies**. To us it isn't supernatural, it is **natural**.

≈ Why does Pappa come to Lapland? What does he do there?
≈ How many of Pappa's brothers and sisters become adults? What happens to the others?

4 conscientious objector:
   person who refuses
   to fight in a war

5 rocker:
   chair that moves back
   and forth

6 reaper:
   1. farm machine
   2. name for death
   (used in both senses in
   this story)

7 birch saplings:
   young trees

8 blood pancakes:
   food made from the
   blood of an animal

9 slaughter:
   killing of a farm animal

10 calved: had a baby (calf)

11 hollered:
   used a loud voice, yelled

12 whoremonger:
   man who pays
   women for sex

13 cussed:
   said bad words, cursed

preached:
spoke about religion

banjo:
a string instrument common
in American folk music

ditch:
lower part on the
side of a road

tuberculosis:
a serious lung disease

diptheria:
a dangerous
contagious disease

crop:
amount of grain, fruit
produced in a season

tore: pulled away

mayor:
most important city official

you can bet:
you can be sure

virgin:
person who has
never had sex

prophecies:
events of the future

natural: usual, normal

≈ Why does Torborg throw her engagement ring on the floor? Who is she like?

≈ What is unusual about the Kell people?

Mamma's older brother Karl went to America when he was eighteen. There he is **chopping** a redwood tree. And there he is working in a gold mine. He married a woman called Viviann, and he visited us in Sweden. Let me tell you, the village had never seen anyone like her. Not only had she been divorced, but she had bobbed[14] hair, wore makeup, and dresses with padded[15] shoulders, matching shoes, and purses. Vanity of all vanities[16] was quoted from the Bible. So of course everyone knew the marriage wouldn't last—besides they didn't have any children. Uncle Karl is now old and fat and the darling and benefactor[17] of a Swedish Old Folks Home in Canada. Silver mines help him. This is Mamma's second brother. He had to have his leg **amputated**. I used to think about that leg, all alone in heaven. This is Aunt Edith. She once gave me a silver spoon that had my name written on it. And this is Aunt Elsa who has a large birthmark[18] on her face. I used to wonder what mark I had to **prove** I was born.

Mamma's father was a Communist. He came to Lapland to build the large power plant that **supplies** most of Sweden's electricity. He told me, once, that he ate snake when he was young and worked on the railroad. His wife Emma was a beauty and a lady, and when the household money permitted, she washed her face with heavy cream and her hair with beer or egg whites. My hair? Both grandmothers had hair long enough to sit on.

I am talking about my **inheritance**—the family jewelry that I wear in my hair, so to speak, the birthmark that stays on my face forever. I am motherless in Lapland, brought down to size[19] by the vastness of the sky. I rock in the rocker of old age and ride the reaper, while some part of me has already **preceded** me to heaven. I change one husband for another, and **toss** my ring, furiously moral at any indignation[20]. I am a **pacifist**, I am a Communist, I am a preacher coddling[21] my father's language and abandoning my mother tongue forever. I eat blood pancakes, calf-dance, snake, and I bring the horse in the kitchen. I build new houses, dream of new dresses, bury my parents and my children. I hear ghosts, see the future and know what will happen. If I step on a crack and break my mother's back[22], I can say the shoes were too large for my feet, for I know, I know: these are **fairy tales** that **grieve** us. And save us.

≈ Describe Viviann. What does the family think of her?

≈ How many brothers and sisters does Mamma have? What do you know about them?

chopping: cutting

amputated: cut off

prove: make certain

supplies: gives, provides

inheritance: what one receives from someone who dies

preceded: went before

toss: throw

pacifist: one who does not believe in military solutions

fairy tales: magical stories for children

grieve: make sad

14 bobbed: cut short

15 padded: with extra material

16 vanity of all vanities: a phrase from the Bible

17 benefactor: one who gives money and support

18 birthmark: permanent mark on the skin

19 brought down to size: brought low, made small

20 indignation: anger against injustice

21 coddling: taking great care of

22 If I step…: children's superstitious saying

≋ Describe Mamma's father and his wife.

≋ How did the narrator get her long hair?

≋ Does the narrator believe that she inherited many different things
from her family? How do you know?

EXPLORING THE STORY

AN ACTIVITY FOR GROUP DISCUSSION, HOMEWORK, OR YOUR JOURNAL

A good writer will not only describe interesting characters and an
interesting plot—what happens in the story—but will also provide extra
ideas or opinions that are not always easy to see.

*Answer the activities and questions below. Always go back to the
story to explain your answers.*

1. Look at the categories below and write down the names of the
persons who fit beneath each word. One name may fit in more
than one category. The first one is done for you.

Appearance

fat _Uncle Karl, Tora_____

makeup _____

amputated _____

Beliefs

conscientious objector _____

religious _____

communist _____

Profession

preached _____

reaper _____

miner _____

engineer _____

Temperament

dream _____

yelled _____

cussed _____

Skills

built _____

banjo _____

ski _____

ghosts _____

2. Which of the words in the above categories also describe the speaker? Explain your answer.

3. The speaker uses information that was given to her and also her own memories. Notice the different phrases the speaker uses to introduce memories and make a list of them. The first one is: *He told me he didn't have any shoes.* Can you find other examples?

4. Choose the sentence that best describes the story:
   a) Knowing your family history helps you understand what is important.
   b) Knowing your family history helps you understand yourself.
   c) Knowing your family history helps you understand the future.

5. What do you think of the title "Family Album?" Can you think of a different title? Give reasons for your answers.

EXPLORING THE VOCABULARY

Complete the following sentences with bold words from the story. Change the form of the word when necessary.

1. The detective _____ to the police who had stolen the money.
2. Isn't it _____ for parents to protect their children?
3. He _____ the ball to the dog.
4. The priest _____ an excellent sermon last Sunday.
5. Because of the war, this year's olive _____ will not be harvested.
6. The _____ gave the keys to the city to the visiting minister.
7. I _____ a ligament in my shoulder when I was playing tennis.
8. He worked for his money. It wasn't his _____.
9. Will you please go into the forest and _____ some wood for the winter?

Now choose ten of the numbered words and write a sentence for each one. You may copy sentences from your dictionary.

EXPLORING THE LANGUAGE

LANGUAGE CHUNKS

Many students like to learn fixed expressions (words that usually go together) and then use these "chunks" of language in speaking or writing. This kind of learning is very common when you learn your first language. We recommend that you learn these language chunks.

Here is a list of chunks from "Family Album." Study them. Unlike the other units in this book, these words are not necessarily defined in the margins; you should know most of them and use this as a review.

from all around	smiling at
step on	brought down to size
look good	died of
dreamed of	tore off

Now complete these sentences with one of the expressions, changing the form of the words when necessary.

1. Every night, he _____ being famous.
2. In his dreams, people would come _____ the world to meet him.
3. Everything he said would be meaningful to their lives, and everyone would be _____ the thought of his words.
4. Wherever he would go, whatever plane he would _____, people would know his name.
5. However, in the morning, reality would always _____ his dreams _____.

EXPLORING THE WRITING

TITLES

The author chooses the *title* carefully to communicate to you what is important in the story. The title can help you, the reader, to focus on what the author is going to say. In this textbook, you will read complete short stories, like "Family Album"; excerpts of longer stories, like "Clothes"; or excerpts from a book. In a book, the chapters may have their own titles; for example, "Spring Love" is a chapter of *House of the Winds*.

The title of this story, "Family Album," gives you immediate information about the story you are about to read. Together, the words suggest a book filled with family photographs. They help you *predict*—know in advance—what the story is about, and making good predictions helps you understand what you are reading. They also prepare you for the way the author is going to tell her story as if she were talking to you, showing you pictures of her family, and answering your questions.

Below are titles of some of the stories in *Views and Voices*. Look at the titles and write down what the words suggest to you. You will know whether you made a good prediction after you have read the stories.

"The Visit" may be about _____.

"Spring Love" may be about _____.

"Clothes" may be about _____.

EXPLORING YOUR IDEAS

AN ACTIVITY FOR GROUP DISCUSSION, HOMEWORK, OR YOUR JOURNAL

Read these sentences from the story and respond with your ideas and feelings. Discuss or write as much as possible because, as you do, more ideas will come to you.

1. … they were always making blueprints together.
2. Three died in a six-week period and Pappa says that death was accepted then…
3. Everyone on this side of the family hears ghosts and dreams prophecies.
4. I used to wonder what mark I had to prove I was born.
5. … these are fairy tales that grieve us. And save us.

EXPLORING THE INTERNET

You will find information on the people who live in Lapland at these sites: **www.itv.se/boreale/samieng.htm** and **www.scandinavica.com/sami.htm**.

Discover one of the leading networks for connecting families, **www.myfamilyinc.com**. Visit the corporation's many sites to create your own family website, search for ancestors, or build a family tree.

Create your own family album, plus organize your family's holidays, recipes, and more at **www.thefamilymemories.com**.

If you are interested in your genealogy (family history), this site may help you get started: **www.genealogy.com**.

In addition to being an author, Siv Cedering is also an artist. At **www.sculpturesite.com/categoryPages/fountains0.html** you'll find some of her sculptures (see the "Siv Cedering" link). What does Siv Cedering's art say to you?

Have you ever thought of cooking snake, bear, or crickets? Find unusual recipes using these ingredients and more at **www.recipecottage.com/misc** (do a recipe search for one of the above!).

We encourage you to do your own Internet search and share the sites you find with your classmates and with your teacher.

FOLLOW-UP ACTIVITIES

Choose one or more of the following activities to complete:

1. Make a family tree for the characters in this story or make your own family tree. Don't be afraid to use your imagination if you don't have much information.
2. Make a drawing or a collage to illustrate this story.
3. Write a paragraph or tell a story about a member of your family who was unusual.
4. Write a short paragraph describing three things that you would like people to know and understand about you and your family.
5. Make a short class presentation or an audiocassette/videotape on one of these topics:
   a) The people of Lapland
   b) How to start your family tree
   c) A recipe for an unusual dish
6. Interview a classmate or an acquaintance about his or her parents or grandparents. Ask where they came from, what they did there, how they looked, and what special interests they had. Then write a paragraph about your friend's family.

If you enjoyed reading "Family Album," we suggest that you read the other stories in the anthology, *Sudden Fiction International.* See the acknowledgements page for publishing information.

Unit

4

THE VISIT
Catherine Lim

Singapore

They only talked of his Mummy when they thought he was asleep and not around…

Unit **4**

THE VISIT
Catherine Lim

Singapore

INTRODUCTION

Think about and/or discuss these questions:

1. When parents divorce, what happens to the children?
   Which parent should they live with?
2. At what age can children be told the truth about divorce?
3. Describe your favorite toys when you were little. Do you know who or what Pooh Bear is?
4. What kind of games and bedtime stories did you enjoy as a child?
   Who played with you?

LIBRARY/INTERNET TASKS

Before you read the story:

1. Find out where Singapore is located, what languages are spoken there, and what the main cultures of Singapore are.
2. Find out why English is commonly used in Singapore.
3. Find out more about Winnie the Pooh (Pooh Bear), a famous character in English children's literature.

The Visit

Catherine Lim

Catherine Lim grew up in Malaysia and lives and writes in Singapore. She is Chinese and her first language is English. An author of many collections of short stories and novels, Catherine Lim's story "The Visit" is from her book *Or Else, The Lightning God and Other Stories*.

The bold words should be learned. The numbered words are explained to help you understand the story. Some words have more than one meaning. The meaning we give is the closest synonym.

Yen Li lay very still on his bed, his eyes tightly closed, his arms around Pooh Bear. He waited for his Daddy and Auntie Poh Har—he must remember to call her Mummy, otherwise his Daddy would have that angry look on his face again—he waited for them to leave the room, for he wanted to be by himself. But they **remained** sitting on his bed, talking in low tones[1] to each other and thinking he was asleep and couldn't hear them. But he heard everything, though he kept his eyes tightly closed and lay **perfectly** still.

remained: stayed

perfectly: completely

1 tones: sounds

2 sobbing: crying loudly

3 clucking:
   making a sound
   with her tongue

They were talking of his Mummy, he knew. They only talked of his Mummy when they thought he was asleep and not around, and once they talked of her when they thought he was out playing in the garden, but all the time he was behind them, in the little space behind the **curtains**, holding Pooh Bear tightly in his arms. He had stopped playing and talking to Pooh Bear when he heard them come into the room, and he had sat very still for the whole time that they were in the room. His Auntie Poh Har was saying, "You're being rather **hard** on the boy, darling," but his Daddy had replied, "No, I want nothing more to do with her, and I don't want her to come within a mile of this house. The boy will soon get over it."

curtains:
cloth over windows

hard: strict

His Daddy had told him, "You have a new Mummy now, Yen Li. She loves you very much," and Auntie Poh Har had **bent down** and softly touched his cheek. He wanted to ask, "Where's my Mummy? Where's my Mummy gone to?" but he knew what the look on his father's face and the tone in his father's voice meant, so he never asked any questions about his mother.

bent down:
bend her body at the
knees or waist

One night in his room, he thought about his Mummy and his eyes filled with tears. He began sobbing[2] on his pillow and the old servant Ah Keem Chae came in (his Daddy and Auntie Poh Har had gone out). Ah Kheem Chae sat with him for a while, saying all sorts of things to make him stop crying. He cried so much that he **threw up**, and Ah Kheem Chae, shaking her head and clucking[3] her tongue, cleaned him and changed his pajamas.

threw up:
vomited, food came up
from the stomach

The next evening, just before dinner, his Daddy came home with a big **parcel wrapped** in shiny red paper, and Auntie Poh Har also had a parcel under her arm. They put the parcels in front of him, smiling and asking him to unwrap them. There was a **handsome**, shiny gun, and a motorcycle. His father showed him how to shoot with the gun and how to make the motorcycle go very fast, and for a while, he played with the toys and did not cry so much. As he was playing with his motorcycle in the kitchen one morning, he heard Ah Kheem Chae talking to Ah Soh, the washerwoman and he knew they were talking of his Mummy, for they both kept turning to look at him, and shaking their heads.

parcel: package

wrapped: covered

handsome: beautiful

What does Yen Li have to call Auntie Poh Har?

When does his father get angry?

How does Yen Li's father feel about the boy's mother?

What does Yen Li's father do to try to make him happy again?

He thought they were saying something bad about his Mummy, and again he wanted to ask, "Where's my Mummy?" but he **did not dare** to, as he knew his father would be angry with him for that.

did not dare: was afraid

Once his Mummy had telephoned him. He was in his room, talking to Pooh Bear, when Ah Kheem Chae called from downstairs in a shrill excited voice, "Yen Li, it's your Mummy! Quick!" He had rushed[4] down the stairs, breathless, clutching[5] Pooh Bear. It was indeed his mother. He didn't even hear what she wanted to tell him, for at the sound of her voice, he had started to cry. He sobbed so miserably[6] that Ah Kheem Chae took over the phone from him and spoke to his mother. By the time he had **recovered** sufficiently[7] to speak to her, his father had come home and could be heard coming out of his car, so Ah Kheem Chae quickly put down the phone and hurried him downstairs.

He wanted his Mummy. He wanted his Mummy to come back to him. Most of all, he wanted his Mummy to come back so they could continue their game with Pooh Bear. It was a game that they had both **invented**. In this game, he would lie under his blanket, and his mother would tell him a story about Pooh Bear, and **act out** Pooh Bear's actions on him, as he lay very **still** under his blanket. His mother would make Pooh Bear walk over his stomach, jump up and down on his head, dig[8] its toes into his ribs. Pooh Bear took on[9] many **roles**—as a hunter[10], fisherman, **robber**, **giant**, crab[11], elephant—and his body, as he lay snugly[12], with the blanket drawn right over his head was the **territory** over which the **hero** roamed[13] and had his **adventures**. But the part Yen Li liked the best was the end of the story, when Pooh Bear invariably[14] returned home to his mother. His Mummy's words, "So Pooh Bear ran and ran and when he saw his Mummy, he **gave her a hug**, hug, hug, and a kiss, kiss, kiss!" were the cue[15] for him to be **released** from the self-imposed immobility[16], and to jump up, throw his arms round her and kiss her resoundingly[17] three times in **faithful** re-enactment[18] of Pooh Bear's homecoming.

Every night he waited for his Mummy to come and say Goodnight and play the game, his little body taut[19] with eager anticipation[20] as he lay under the blanket. All his **senses** were strained[21] to catch the **magical** words at the end of the story, and the moment the first 'hug' was uttered[22]. He sprang up[23] with the agility[24] of a monkey and flung[25] himself into his mother's arms, covering her with kisses.

Now his Mummy had gone away, and she hadn't even finished the last story. He remembered it clearly. Pooh Bear was climbing a mountain in search of a house full of gold coins. His head was Pooh Bear's mountain, and he giggled[26] convulsively[27], though he was **supposed to** lie very still, when he felt the bear's feet moving all over his face.

His mother was halfway through the story when his father came into the room. There was an angry look on his father's face. He heard his father shouting at his mother; she got up from the bed, and stood there, shouting back at him. Then they left the room. He could hear

recovered:
become well again

invented: made up, created

act out: perform, do

still: quietly

roles: actor's part in a play

robber: person who steals

giant: very large, tall person

territory: area

hero: brave one

adventures:
exciting or dangerous experiences

gave her a hug:
put his arms around her

released: freed

faithful: exact

senses:
sight/seeing, smell, taste, hearing, touch

magical: wonderful

supposed to: should

4 rushed: run fast

5 clutching: holding

6 miserably: sadly

7 sufficiently: enough

8 dig: push, poke

9 took on: played

10 hunter:
   one who catches and kills animals

11 crab: a sea animal

12 snugly:
   warmly, comfortably

13 roamed: traveled

14 invariably: always

15 cue: sign, signal

16 self-imposed immobility:
   chosen stillness

17 resoundingly: loudly

18 re-enactment:
   replay, repetition

19 taut: tight, stiff

20 eager anticipation:
   great excitement

21 strained: trying hard

22 uttered: said

23 sprang up: jumped

24 agility: quickness

25 flung: threw

26 giggled: laughed

27 convulsively: strongly

28 air conditioner: cooling machine

29 pretended to be: made believe he was

30 fearfully: with fear

31 dreadful: very bad, terrible

32 tractor: farm vehicle

33 quivered: shook

34 pining away: sick with sadness

35 state: condition

36 expectation: hope

37 swept: picked him up

them still shouting at each other, as he lay very still on his bed, his eyes wide open in the darkness. Soon Ah Kheem Chae came in, and she turned off the air-conditioner[28] in his room, as she always did when it started to rain. She moved softly towards his bed and bent down to make sure he was asleep. He pretended to be[29] asleep. But his little heart was beating fearfully[30], for he knew something dreadful[31] was happening.

🐦 Was Yen Li able to talk to his mother on the telephone?
🐦 Describe the game that Yen Li loves.
🐦 What happens at the end of the game?
🐦 What happens between his parents to upset Yen Li so much?
🐦 Who takes care of Yen Li except for his mother?

The next morning his father called him and said that his mother had gone away; she would not be coming back, and when his eyes filled with tears, his father said, "Don't cry, son, for God's sake, don't cry." Later that afternoon, his father bought him a toy tractor[32], but his little heart was too heavy to play with anything; he wanted his Mummy.

He couldn't eat, and when he thought no one was looking, his lips quivered[33] and the tears would come again. He wanted his mother **especially** at night; he wanted her to continue the story of Pooh Bear. He waited a long time but his mother did not come back.

especially: mainly, mostly

When he lay ill in bed, he heard Auntie Poh Har (he must remember to call her Mummy) say to his father, "You must **allow** him to see her at least once, darling. Look the child's pining away[34]," and then he heard his father say, "Let him get better first. I don't want him to be **upset** while in this state[35]."

allow: permit, agree to

upset: sad, worried

And now his Mummy was coming! He had been told by his father and Auntie Poh Har that his Mummy would be coming for a short visit. It was true, for he heard them talking about it again, as he lay pretending to be asleep, while they sat on his bed.

"Let it be over with," he heard his father say, and add, "the boy should be told the truth one of these days. Then his eyes will be opened." He heard Auntie Poh Har say, "He's only a child, darling. You mustn't be too hard on him."

Yen Li waited, clutching Pooh Bear, his little body **tense** with expectation[36]. His Daddy and Auntie Poh Har were out. Ah Kheem Chae was in the kitchen. He heard the sound of a car in the drive. He leapt from his seat and ran to the door. He saw his mother getting out of the car, and was about to rush to her when he saw her turn to speak to somebody who had got out of the car with her. He was a tall man, much taller than his Daddy. His mother then saw him, rushed to him, swept[37] him up in her arms and held him very tight.

tense: stiff, tight

"My little son," she said, her face glowing[38] with joy, and she turned to the man and said, "This is the Yen Li I've been speaking to you about," and the man said, "Fine boy," and then looked around the place, commenting[39] that it was a fine house and garden.

"Yen Li, this is Uncle Bill, say 'hello' to Uncle Bill, darling," she coaxed[40], leading the boy forward to where Uncle Bill had seated himself. Yen Li said 'Hello' very **shyly**, and then abruptly[41] turned to his mother and clung[42] to her. She drew him close to her again and kissed him. Then, still holding him in her arms, she turned to Uncle Bill and said, "They wouldn't let me see him, darling. They wouldn't let me see my own son. This visit was practically[43] forced out[44] of them. My own little Yen Li," she said again and again, ruffling[45] his hair.

- How does Yen Li's father expect him to behave?
- How do we know that Yen Li is very unhappy?
- Do his father and stepmother agree on when Yen Li will see his mother again?
- Who comes to see Yen Li with his mother?
- What do you know about Uncle Bill?

He would have liked to **drag** her upstairs by the hand to make her continue the game with Pooh Bear, to have her all to himself, but she was talking to Uncle Bill all the time as she held him close to her. At one point, she moved over to sit very close to Uncle Bill and put her head on his shoulder, **sighing**, "I'm happy at last, Bill. Nobody can take this happiness away from me." Then she went back to sit with Yen Li and she put her face against his murmuring[46], "Mummy's very happy at last, darling. Aren't you glad that your Mummy is happy at last?"

Yen Li wanted to ask, "When is Uncle Bill going off? I want you to come upstairs with me so that we can play with Pooh Bear!" but started crying instead. He sobbed[47] loud and long, his little body convulsed[48] with the pain of it all. His mother tried to comfort him.

"Ssh, silly, silly boy," she said stroking[49] his hair. "You love Mummy very much, don't you? Never mind, **sweetheart**, Uncle Bill and I will be coming to see you again. Won't we, Uncle Bill? And Uncle Bill said in a **cheerful,** booming[50] voice, "Of course[51], of course. We're going to Europe soon, boy, and we'll come to see you directly[52] when we return. Okay, sonny? And he continued to look around the house, saying, for the second time, "Mmm, fine place, this."

Yen Li, his eyes brimming[53] with tears, **managed** to say, between sobs, "Pooh Bear." His mother looked **puzzled** then noticing the rumpled[54] bear in his arms, leaned back and laughed, "Of course,

shyly: without confidence

drag: pull

sighing: breathing heavily with relief

sweetheart: loved one

cheerful: happy

managed: was able to

puzzled: not understanding, confused

38 glowing: shining

39 commenting: saying, stating

40 coaxed: talked sweetly, persuaded

41 abruptly: suddenly

42 clung: held on tight

43 practically: almost

44 forced out: pulled out

45 ruffling: playing with

46 murmuring: speaking softly

47 sobbed: cried loudly

48 convulsed: shook

49 stroking: touching gently

50 booming: very loud

51 of course: clearly

52 directly: soon

53 brimming: filled with

54 rumpled: worn, well-loved

55 inseparable:
    unable to be parted

56 entertained:
    amused, pleased

57 no end: a lot, very much

58 conspiratorially:
    in a secret way

59 crept: moved very quietly

60 trussed up: thrown away

sweetheart! Pooh Bear—your favorite toy. I shall get you a bigger one when I return from Europe, darling, much bigger and nicer than this one. Poor thing, one of its eyes is falling out." She tried to fix it back, gave up, and turned to Uncle Bill, laughing, "His favorite toy, darling. Inseparable⁵⁵. I used to **amuse** him for hours with it. Silly little game that entertained⁵⁶ him no end⁵⁷."

amuse: have fun with

When it was time for her to go, she hugged him close and promised to write to him from Europe.

"We'll send you postcards, sweetheart, only to you, no one else," she said conspiratorially⁵⁸ and Uncle Bill said, "Bye, sonny, be a good boy," and then they were gone.

Yen Li went up to his room and crept⁵⁹ into bed. He lay still a long time and then fell asleep. When his Daddy and Auntie Poh Har came back, he was awake, but he pretended to be asleep when they came into his room and stood by his bed. His father saw Pooh Bear in a corner where it had been flung in anger so that it lay trussed up⁶⁰ in an untidy heap. Picking it up, he **gently** put it back in the arms of the sleeping boy.

gently: kindly and carefully

ᔐ How does Yen Li's mother feel?
ᔐ What does Yen Li want his mother to do with him?
ᔐ How does Yen Li feel about Uncle Bill?
ᔐ Where is his mother going?
ᔐ What does the father do to show that he cares about his son?

EXPLORING THE STORY

AN ACTIVITY FOR GROUP DISCUSSION, HOMEWORK, OR YOUR JOURNAL

A good writer will not only describe interesting characters and an interesting plot—what happens in the story—but will also provide extra ideas or opinions that are not always easy to see.

Answer the following activities and questions. Always go back to the story to find the answers to the questions.

1. There are six characters in "The Visit." Look at the adjectives below and on the next page and write the name of the character that fits the description and the sentence in the text that supports it. Adjectives may fit more than one character.

    Cruel _____

    Understanding _____

    Betrayed _____

Angry _____

Lonely _____

Loving _____

Indifferent _____

Vulnerable _____

Secretive _____

Controlling _____

Kind _____

2. What do the phrases "very still," "they thought he was asleep,"
   "they thought he wasn't around," and "he pretended to be asleep"
   tell you about Yen Li and the adults around him?

3. What does Pooh Bear represent for Yen Li? Why does he throw the
   bear across the room after his mother's visit?

4. The central character of the story is Yen Li. How would the author's
   message change if she had chosen to tell the story from another
   character's point of view? Give some examples.

5. In what way did your feelings for the characters change as you
   read the story? Give examples.

6. What indications do you get from the text that Uncle Bill is not
   Chinese?

7. Why do you think the author called this story "The Visit?" Can you
   think of other titles for this story?

EXPLORING THE VOCABULARY

Complete the following sentences with bold words from the story.
Change the form of the word when necessary.

1. The teacher told the students who came late to
   _____ after class.

2. The boy _____ his friend to jump off the roof.

3. The gift was _____ in bright red paper.

4. Many people I know think that Nelson Mandela is a modern

   _____.

5. Parents are not _____ do their children's homework for them in some countries.

6. Let's _____ that we are very rich and can buy
   whatever we want.

7. I was most _____ when he didn't phone after he
   said he would.

8. From the mountains to the ocean, they went on many
   _____ together.
9. You look so _____. Did you win the lottery?
10. My little girl _____ to tie her shoelaces for the
    first time.
11. The scientists were always _____ new ways
    to do things.

*Now choose ten of the numbered words and write a sentence for
each one. You may copy sentences from your dictionary.*

EXPLORING THE LANGUAGE

LANGUAGE CHUNKS

Many students like to learn fixed expressions (words that usually go
together) and then use these "chunks" of language in speaking or writing.
This kind of learning is very common when you learn your first language.
We recommend that you learn these language chunks.

*Here is a list of chunks from "The Visit." Study them. They are
explained in the margins of the story.*

the whole time	get over
bent down	throw up
shake your head	put down
come back	act out
jump up and down	spring up
in search of	shouting at
wide open	turn off
at least	play with
of course	fall out
give up	no end
fall asleep	in anger

*Now complete these sentences with one of the expressions, chang-
ing the form of the words when necessary.*

1. You need to _____ to fasten your shoelaces.
2. Sometimes you feel better after you _____.
3. At the end of the test, the examiner told them to
   _____ their pens and pencils.
4. The dentist told me to keep my mouth _____.
5. I don't want to _____ you any more.
   You're too rough.

6. After her husband died, it took her a long time to
_____ her loss.
7. In some countries, like Romania, when you _____
it means yes.
8. They forgot to pay for their food, and the waiter ran after them
and told them to _____.
9. _____ the lights when you leave the room.
10. Mary _____ of her bed because it was too small.

EXPLORING THE WRITING

FICTION

Writing can be divided into two large groups: *non-fiction* and *fiction*.
Examples of non-fiction include books or other writings on politics,
science, travel, or biographies. The information in these books is based
on facts and real events, and the information can be checked.

Fiction describes writing of the imagination, the ideas and pictures
that come into someone's head. In fiction, the *author*—the person who
writes the book—can create any story he or she likes. Names, places,
events, all come from the author's own ideas. The author has complete
freedom in a work of fiction. One of the important choices an author
makes is to decide how the story is told.

Sometimes, there is a first-person *narrator*—a character in the book
who uses "I" to tell the story. It is important for you to know that "I" is
not necessarily the author, only a character in a story. Examples are
units 5 and 8.

In other cases, the author may choose a central character in his or her
story and use "he" or "she." This unit is a good example. Catherine Lim
chooses the little boy as her main character and uses "he." Unit 1 is
another example.

Finally, the author may tell his or her story through different characters
without choosing any of them in particular. This is the case of units 11
and 12. For some more information on types of writing, see Unit 7.

EXPLORING YOUR IDEAS

AN ACTIVITY FOR GROUP DISCUSSION, HOMEWORK, OR YOUR JOURNAL

Read these sentences from the story and respond with your ideas and feelings. Discuss or write as much as possible because, as you do, more ideas will come to you.

1. "No, I want nothing more to do with her and I don't want her coming within a mile of this house. The boy will soon get over it."
2. "Silly little game that entertained him to no end."
3. "Aren't you glad Mummy is happy at last?"
4. Picking it up, he gently put it back in the arms of the sleeping boy.

EXPLORING THE INTERNET

As are families, so is society. You'll find this quote and more insights into families and divorce laws at the Family Court of Singapore's site, **www.familycourtofsingapore.gov.sg**. Specific information on divorce laws in Singapore can be found at **www.lawsociety.org.sg/html/awareness/divorce.htm**.

For a deeper understanding of family values in Singapore, explore the site of the Singapore-based organization, About Family Life, at **www.aboutfamilylife.org.sg**. A site search using the keyword "divorce" will connect you with resources to dealing with the issue.

At **www.sg**, you'll discover a world of information about Singapore. See "Our Shared Values" under the "Flavours of Singapore" link for an insight into family values in Singapore. Also see the link to **www.sg/kids** to view Singapore through a child's eyes.

Why is Winnie the Pooh such a beloved bear?
Visit **www.just-pooh.com/home.html** to read the history of Pooh and his friends. You can even play a game to help Pooh gather honey!

To learn more about famous characters in children's literature in English, you can find links to some classic stories at **www.ucalgary.ca/~dkbrown/storclas.html**.

Would you like to know if you have a lucky name according to the *I Ching?* Try **www.chinesefortunecalendar.com/luckyname12.htm**.

Why do children create imaginary friends? You'll find one explanation at **health.discovery.com/expert/yale/family/imaginary.html**.

We encourage you to do your own Internet search and share the sites you find with your classmates and with your teacher.

FOLLOW-UP ACTIVITIES

Choose one or more of the following activities to complete:

1. The story "The Visit" is set in Singapore. Either write a composition or give a talk about the country. Try to find pictures to illustrate your work. If possible, find information on the Internet or in the library.
2. Write a dialogue in which a parent tells his or her son or daughter that there will be a divorce in the family.
3. In some countries, after a divorce, the court may decide to award joint custody to both parents. Find out about this and decide if you are in favor or not. Either write about the situation or give a talk.
4. Illustrate a scene from "The Visit."
5. A. A. Milne is the author of books about "Winnie the Pooh." Find out about the books or the author. Either write or talk about your research.
6. Write your reactions to the story in your journal.
7. Retell the story as though you were Poh Har or Ah Kheem Chae.

If you enjoyed reading this story by Catherine Lim, we suggest that you read the other stories in her book, *Or Else, The Lightening God, and Other Stories.* See the acknowledgements page for publishing information.

Unit
5

SPRING LOVE

Mia Yun

Korea

Sister was nineteen and in love with this bulldog-faced man.

Korea

Unit **5**

SPRING LOVE
Mia Yun

INTRODUCTION

Think about and/or discuss these questions:

1. When you meet new people, do you decide quickly how you feel about them or do you prefer to take some time to get to know them first?
2. Have you ever changed your opinion of someone after knowing the person better? In what way?
3. What is the difference between liking someone and being in love with someone?
4. What kind of singing voice do you like?
5. What are the names of some famous singers in your country? Talk about your favorite singer.
6. What are the positive and negative sides of an artistic career?

LIBRARY/INTERNET TASKS

Before you read the story:

1. Find information about Korea and Korean culture.
2. Look for information about opera. If possible, listen to a piece of operatic music.

SPRING LOVE

Mia Yun

Mia Yun was born in Korea where she lived until she went to the United States as a young adult. She received a Master of Fine Arts degree from City College of New York and is a journalist and a free-lance writer. "Spring Love" is Chapter 12 from her first novel, *House of the Winds.*

The bold words should be learned. The numbered words are explained to help you understand the story. Some words have more than one meaning. The meaning we give is the closest synonym.

There was a certain section of the street I passed every afternoon returning home from school. It came at the trailing end[1] of a commercial strip[2] where the paving work[3] ended abruptly. It was a dry spring and rain that always left deep potholes there rarely came. Instead, there hung a hazy[4] film of dust in the air. All day long, fine dust rained and landed on the three shabby[5] buildings standing there side by side in commiseration[6].

1 trailing end: very end

2 commercial strip: row of businesses

3 paving work: finished surface of a road

4 hazy: cloudy

5 shabby: old and worn

6 commiseration: shared sadness, sympathy

Although nobody ever noticed it, the building in the middle was an animal hospital. By now the **carelessly** painted sign—black calligraphy swirls[7]—hanging on top of the building, "North Mountain Animal Hospital" had **faded** into the gray background. The interior was always as dark as a cave as the sun failed to **penetrate** the windows, caked with[8] years of dust and grime[9].

Several times when there was no one around, I had pressed my face to the window, holding my hand to shield[10] the sunlight and **peered** inside. Along a wall stood cages—rusting[11] and skeletal[12]—that held a few scrappy[13], dispirited[14] **puppies** and a couple of sleepy cats. Against the other side of the wall, below colored and fading pictures of animals—dogs with bones and rabbits chewing on cabbages—stood an old dilapidated[15] piano, its wood chipping[16]. There sat the mystery man—the man that sister was in love with—playing the piano and singing in his steely[17] **tenor** voice. Korean arias[18] and ariettas[18]. Sometimes, I would recognize a familiar aria from an Italian opera. Was it from the *Barber of Seville* or from *Rigoletto*[19]? I don't remember.

At other times, I saw him carrying a dented **tin** bucket outside the hospital. He was a big imposing[20] figure in blue denim **overalls**. He looked like an American farmer in Arkansas[21] I had seen in a magazine. He had a tenor's paunch[22] which he carried like a badge of honor[23], something I would see later in Luciano Pavarotti[24]. I quickly hurried by him as if I had no business being there spying on[25] him, stealing a look at his **impressive** bulldog[26] face.

Sister was nineteen and in love with this bulldog-faced man. She looked up to him. She **idolized** him. He was the guru[27] of her new **faith**. She believed what this man believed—that he was the best tenor Korea had ever produced. Wait and see. Time would prove that. In his dreams, he often stood with a flowing kerchief[28] in his hand at the center of the **stage** at Carnegie Hall or Lincoln Center or La Scala[29]. The cheers from the adulating[30] crowd in front of him were deafening. Moved[31], he **wept**. But for now, this man, older than sister by more than a **decade**, honed the tool[32] for his fame at a dusty animal hospital in a suburb of Seoul. And sister was in love with him.

⊘ Describe the animal hospital.
⊘ Why is the narrator looking inside the animal hospital?
⊘ Who is in love?
⊘ What do you know about the mystery man?

carelessly: without care

faded: become pale with age
penetrate: enter

peered: looked closely

puppies: young dogs

tenor:
high male adult voice

tin: silvery metal
overalls:
work pants with a
front piece

impressive: large, important

idolized:
loved with total
admiration

faith: religion

stage:
raised area in front
of the public in a theater

wept: cried

decade: ten years

raced: ran very fast

conductor: person who directs the music

soloist: singer who sings alone

choir: group of singers

soprano: high female voice

approving: pleased, accepting

chick: baby bird

bloomed: opened like a flower

limit: end

urged: advised strongly

encouraged her: gave her courage

chanting: repeating

mold: form, shape

Christmas Eve: night before Christmas

robe: long, loose clothing

eagle: very large bird

impressed: admiring

ambitions: goals

heroic: very brave

Three evenings a week, sister **raced** to her church where he was a **conductor** and **soloist** for the church **choir** and sang in her soaring[33] **soprano** under his **approving** eyes. She was a **chick** dreaming of her first flight under his protective wing. Under his attention, she **bloomed** and bloomed each day as if there was no **limit** to how far a girl could go on blooming. She was beautiful in her love.

He **urged** sister to take up new piano lessons, to learn how to breathe properly and how to project[34] her already beautiful voice. This man **encouraged her**, inspired[35] her and cheered her on to sing better, better than anybody. This man blew his dreams in her soul. One day, he told her again and again like a man **chanting** a holy mantra[36], together they would build a flourishing[37] career as a soprano and a tenor in Italy and America. The world would be theirs to **mold** as if it were a ball of soft clay[38] in the hand. Sister believed it. That was what she wanted, what she dreamed of and hoped for: a life of music with him.

On **Christmas Eve**, mother went to the church to sneak a look at[39] him. The man her daughter was so in love with. Mother took a seat in an inconspicuous[40] corner and watched him conduct the church choir in a beautiful rendering[41] of Handel's *Messiah*[42]. In his flowing church **robe**, he looked like a spreading[43], soaring **eagle**. Built so big and solid and imposing as an oak tree. How **impressed** mother was with him! In contrast[44], her daughter, in the front of the choir, looked like a child. Her mouth open wide in a big O, belching out[45] her voice in such earnestness[46]! She couldn't help but smile.

At midnight, the church choir showed up outside the gate of our house. We ran to the window and watched them stand in the snow drift[47] and sing. How they cheerfully blasted[48] the calm of the snowy night with "Joy to the World!" They followed it with "The Holy City," our favorite. After the last song, "O Holy Night" was sung, Mother invited them inside and treated them to scalding[49] tea and red bean cakes.

⊘ What is sister's dream?

⊘ Where did mother go on Christmas Eve? What did she see?

⊘ What happened at midnight?

That night on the eve of Christmas, mother saw this man sister loved was not a shy man. He was a man as confident as a bullfighter. A man of conceit[50] and self-assurance. He heartily consumed[51] five red bean cakes and downed two cups of tea. When he spoke, his voice was pleasing to the ear as a glazed candy[52] on a tongue. He praised sister in glowing words and spoke of his **ambitions** with **heroic** charm. Mother

33 soaring: rising high

34 project: send forward

35 inspired: gave her confidence

36 holy mantra: religious words

37 flourishing: successful

38 clay: soft earth

39 sneak a look at: try to look secretly

40 inconspicuous: not easy to notice

41 rendering: performance

42 Handel's *Messiah*: famous religious music

43 spreading: wide

44 in contrast: on the contrary

45 belching out: raising

46 earnestness: seriousness

47 snow drift: pile of snow

48 blasted: put an end to

49 scalding: boiling hot

50 conceit: great opinion of himself

51 heartily consumed: hungrily ate

52 glazed candy: shiny piece of sugar

53 ego: opinion of himself

54 out of proportion: not balanced

55 neglected: paid no attention to

56 training: education

57 debut: first public

58 lamé gown: formal dress

59 pumps: formal shoes

60 frosted: silvery

61 Diana Ross: American pop singer

62 record jacket: cover for a music album

63 bill: program

64 suspicion: lack of trust

65 dashed: lost, crushed

66 empty promises: false promises

67 forged portraits: false pictures

68 futile attempts: useless efforts

69 peeped: looked closely

70 lilting: singing sweetly

71 impassioned plea: emotional request

72 I shall win: line from a famous opera

73 Una furtiva lacrima (Italian): A secret tear

74 lavish melodies: rich music

75 satin scarf: shiny material worn around the neck

76 fluttering: flying gently

easily saw that this man was a dreamer like her husband. A man who knew how to use words like her husband. A man who **aimed at** something big, bigger than life. A man whose ego[53] was out of proportion[54]. A man who was so much older than her daughter, as her husband had been for her. A man with a mountain-sized ambition and an empty pocket. A man who neglected[55] his university training[56] as a **veterinarian** for **fame** in an unknown world. A man who dreamed and dreamed.

The night "Oratorio Company" held its debut[57] concert in a downtown theater, in the middle of the front row, sister stood in a silver lamé gown[58] and matching pumps[59]. With her teased up hair—the end had been curled out and upward—and frosted[60] pink lips, she looked like Diana Ross[61] on the record jacket[62] of the Supremes.

On the music bill[63] mother saved was his picture: a bulldog with **fiery** eyes. He was the **founder** and artistic director of "Oratorio Company." Mother always said, "**Titles** don't make a man." We looked at the music bill with the same suspicion[64] we did at father's new business cards where father's name was always accompanied by an impressive title: a president, a managing director or a chief **executive**. Those cards we later came upon in the corners of drawers spoke to us of broken dreams, dashed[65] hopes and empty promises[66]. Father's business cards were forged portraits[67]. Futile attempts[68] at an identity, a **status**. And was this man, we wondered, the other side of the same coin.

One brilliant, windy spring afternoon, I passed by the hospital and found the door locked and closed. I peeped[69] into the dark. There was no one. No yapping dogs. No sleepy cats. The dilapidated piano, though, was still there, standing in the same corner, closed shut and covered thick with fine dust. I could almost hear his voice lilting[70] in Italian. The impassioned plea[71] he used to **spit out** like fire from his mouth! "I shall win! I shall win[72]!" I had been his best audience. I still remembered the afternoon I had first heard him sing *Una furtiva lacrima!*[73] I didn't have to know what these words meant. All the way home that day, the sad and lavish melodies[74] had followed me like a long white satin scarf[75] fluttering[76] in the wind.

⊘ What is mother's impression of the tenor?
⊘ Why are mother and the narrator suspicious?
⊘ How did the animal hospital look in spring?

Another day, I noticed the rusty sign was missing. And inside there was nothing but empty cages and the fading pictures on the wall. The dilapidated piano was also gone and in its place an empty chair stood

aimed at: tried to reach

veterinarian: doctor for animals

fame: public success

fiery: like fire

founder: organizer, creator

titles: names of profession and position

executive: manager

status: position in society

spit out: blow saliva out of the mouth

with a leg missing. So I knew it was true: he was marrying that long-faced girl, a member of the church choir. She and sister had been "sisters in faith[77]." Grandmother had always **preached to** us: there are no friends like "friends in faith."

But did he love this girl? Did he share his dreams and **soul** with her as he had done with sister? He wasn't a fool. The girl's rich family was promising him a future in America. He must have said to himself: "Finally, a chance to have a go at my dream!" And he must have felt that he was closer than ever before to the stages at Carnegie Hall and Lincoln Center and La Scala. **Eagerly** and zealously[78], he **grabbed** the chance. Why not? He lived to sing. He expected sister to understand that. He wouldn't have sacrificed[79] his ambition and his ego for mere love[80]. And he wasn't the first or the last man not to follow his heart.

On the way home from school, I still passed the animal hospital, now closed up and padlocked[81]. I wanted to see him **blush**, **stammer** and crumble[82] in **shame**. I wanted to stand in front of him face to face and spit and walk away although I had been taught never to spit at anyone. And I knew I wouldn't be able to say a word even if I had come across him. I was a shy girl. A polite girl. Just like mother. Still, I couldn't help wanting to spit at this man. But I never came across him nor his shadow. I wondered if it were true, the words in a popular song: "Love could easily become the **root of hatred**."

Sister was inconsolable[83] after that. Like a **cactus** flower that blooms just one night a year, she had bloomed briefly and gorgeously[84] in her love and now stood in front of a world withered and wan[85]. Another star of her life had fallen, **crashed** and burned to **ashes**. This man she had loved, idolized and hoped to build her life with had turned around and walked away. As if nothing had happened. That spring, sister stopped believing what she had always believed, "Ask, and it shall be given to you; **seek**, and you shall find; knock, and it shall be opened unto you." Grandmother's favorite phrase from the **Holy Bible**.

⊘ What do you know of sister's "sister in faith?"
⊘ What choice did the tenor make?
⊘ What does the narrator want to do?
⊘ How is sister changed?

preached to: taught

soul:
center of emotion and thought

eagerly: willingly

grabbed: took quickly

blush: turn red in the face

stammer:
speak with stops and repetitions

shame:
feeling of being a very bad person

root of hatred:
cause of intense dislike

cactus: desert plant

crashed:
broken to pieces, shattered

ashes:
gray powder after a fire

seek: look for, try to find

Holy Bible:
religious book of Christians and Jews

77 sisters in faith:
close friends in the same religion

78 zealously:
intensely, enthusiastically

79 sacrificed:
given up, abandoned

80 for mere love: just for love

81 padlocked:
closed with a heavy, removable lock

82 crumble: fall to pieces

83 inconsolable: forever sad

84 gorgeously: beautifully

85 withered and wan:
dry and pale

EXPLORING THE STORY

AN ACTIVITY FOR GROUP DISCUSSION, HOMEWORK, OR YOUR JOURNAL

A good writer will not only have interesting characters and an interesting plot—what happens in the story—but will also provide extra ideas or opinions that are not always easy to see.

Read the questions below and think about them. Always go back to the story to explain your answers.

1. Read the first three paragraphs of the story. What mood do they set for the story?
2. How would your response to the story be different if the characters had names instead of being called "sister" or "mother," for example? The narrator uses phrases such as "the mystery man" and "this man." What are some other phrases? Do they affect the way you imagine the character? Explain your answer.
3. The father is absent during this time, but he is an important part of the family. What do we learn about him? What kind of a person is he? How does his family think about him? Why might he be away from home? Does his family miss him? In what ways is he similar to the tenor?
4. The narrator of "Spring Love" observes and describes events as she sees them. What do we know about her own feelings for the tenor? How do these change over time? Why?

EXPLORING THE VOCABULARY

Complete the following sentences with bold words from the story. Change the form of the word when necessary.

1. Our daughter, Diana, wants to go on the _____.
   We would prefer her to choose a more stable profession.
2. We _____ her to study nursing or accounting, which are more secure.
3. Diana doesn't care about _____. She wants

   _____.

4. We've heard of so many young people whose careers on the stage have _____.
5. Her grandparents, however, are _____. They

   _____ Diana because they believe she's talented.
6. When I was young, I also had _____. Instead, I married early and raised a family.

7. At that time, I welcomed marriage _____.
   I wanted a husband and children more than anything else.
8. Many young people today _____ different answers.
9. They don't listen when we _____ the old advice.
10. In the end, we will try not to _____ Diana, but
    be there for her whatever she decides.

*Now choose ten of the numbered words and write a sentence for
each one. You may copy sentences from your dictionary.*

EXPLORING THE LANGUAGE

LANGUAGE CHUNKS

Many students like to learn fixed expressions (words that usually go
together) and then use these "chunks" of language in speaking or writing.
This kind of learning is very common when you learn your first language.
We recommend that you learn these language chunks.

*Here is a list of chunks from "Spring Love." Study them. They are
explained in the margins of the story.*

faded into	caked with
badge of honor	spying on
sneak a look at	snow drift
aimed at	out of proportion
empty promises	

*Now complete these sentences with one of the expressions, changing
the form of the words when necessary.*

1. The new family built a white wall around their house that looked
   like a huge _____.
2. The wall was certainly _____ with the rest of
   the houses on the street; the other houses only had small trees
   around them.
3. Why the big wall? Everyone wondered. Is the family afraid of people
   _____ them?
4. Over time, the wall became _____ dirt and the
   white paint _____ the stone, so the family built
   another wall.
5. Finally someone asked, "Why don't you _____
   taking down walls instead of building them?"

EXPLORING THE WRITING

SIMILES AND METAPHORS

Writers use descriptions and comparisons to help our imaginations. This is an example of a description: *The music was beautiful.* Some types of descriptions and comparisons have special names.

Similes describe people, objects, or actions by comparing them with other things or persons and using the words "as" or "like":
The members of the choir sang *like angels.*
The soprano's voice was *as sweet as a bird's song.*

Metaphors do not use the words "as" or "like":
His words of love were *music to her ears.*
The train's whistle *screamed in the silent night.*

Read the sentences below and next to the sentence write
S (simile) or M (metaphor).

1. The interior was always as dark as a cave ... ___
2. He looked like an American farmer in Arkansas ... ___
3. She was a chick dreaming of her first flight under his protective wing. ___
4. This man blew his dreams in her soul. ___
5. Built so big and solid and imposing as an oak tree. ___
6. ...they cheerfully blasted the calm of the snowy night. ___
7. He was a man as confident as a bullfighter. ___

Now read the story again and find one example of each type of comparison that refers to sister.

Simile: _____

Metaphor: _____

Write your own simile and metaphor about a character in "Spring Love."

Simile: _____

Metaphor: _____

EXPLORING YOUR IDEAS

AN ACTIVITY FOR GROUP DISCUSSION, HOMEWORK, OR YOUR JOURNAL

Read these sentences from the story and respond with your ideas and feelings. Discuss or write as much as possible because, as you do, more ideas will come to you.

1. He was the guru of her new faith.
2. She bloomed and bloomed each day...there was no limit to how far a girl could go on blooming.
3. "Titles don't make a man."
4. He wasn't the first or last man not to follow his heart.
5. I was a shy girl. A polite girl. Just like mother.

EXPLORING THE INTERNET

For beautiful pictures and short movies of Korea, go to: **www.knto.or.kr**. The site has good links to information on Korean culture. There is an especially interesting explanation of Korean writing.

For descriptions of operas and links to the sites of opera singers, go to **www.operaam.org**. You can learn something about the history of opera, operatic careers, and the different types of voices at **www.sfopera.com**.

Discover Mia Yun's inspiration for writing in an interview with her at **www.ivillage.com/books/print/0,11873,22612,00.html**.

Can falling in love make a person crazy? Read interesting scientific research on love at **news.bbc.co.uk/1/hi/sci/tech/407125.stm** and listen to a radio excerpt on the subject. Don't miss the "Relevant Stories" section as well!

How do you say "I love you" in different languages? See **www.siamweb.org/content/Romance/172/iluvu_eng.php**.

The "hip" site, **www.yellohgirls.com**, gives teenage girls of Asian descent opportunities to explore their identity and culture. See the "warrior women" link for a list of women who have made an impact through literature and the arts.

We encourage you to do your own Internet search and share the sites you find with your classmates and with your teacher.

FOLLOW-UP ACTIVITIES

Choose one or more of the following activities to complete:

1. Illustrate a scene from "Spring Love."
2. Write a love poem or a song from sister to the tenor, or on a topic of your choice.
3. Write a dialogue between the tenor and a narrator who expresses her real feelings to him.
4. Write a scene between sister and the tenor as they meet for the last time.
5. Find information on one of the following:
   a) *The Barber of Seville* or *Rigoletto*
   b) Luciano Pavarotti
   c) Different types of operatic voices
   Present your information to your classmates in an essay or on an audio cassette.
6. Interview three people about their first love. Write an essay describing the similarities and the differences in their experiences.
7. Project yourself ten years into the future: how do you imagine the life of the tenor to be? And sister's life?
8. Think about your own career plans. Are you satisfied or do you dream of something else? Explain your answer.
9. Interview someone who has chosen an artistic career.
   Ask him or her:
   How old he or she was when he or she decided on a career in the arts.
   If he or she ever considered another career. Why or why not?
   Whether he or she is satisfied with the choice. Why or why not?
   Add two questions of your own. Report the results of your interview in an oral presentation or an essay.

If you enjoyed reading this chapter from Mia Yun's novel, we suggest that you read the whole book *House of the Winds*. See the acknowledgements page for publishing information.

Unit
6

FASTING, FEASTING
Anita Desai

India

Unit
7

POOR VISITOR
Jamaica Kincaid

Antigua
and the USA

Unit
8

ABOUT THE WEDDING FEAST
Ama Ata Aidoo

Ghana

**P
A
R
T

T
W
O**

Unit
9

CLOTHES
Chitra Banerjee Divakaruni

India
and the USA

Unit
10

SECOND CLASS CITIZEN
Buchi Emecheta

Nigeria
and the United Kingdom

Into Adulthood

"You are beautiful." His voice starts a flutter in my belly.
Chitra Banerjee Divakaruni, Clothes

Unit 6

FASTING, FEASTING
Anita Desai

India

'But she works all the time!' Dr Dutt exclaimed…
'At home. Now you must give her a chance to work outside—'

Unit
6

FASTING, FEASTING
Anita Desai

India

INTRODUCTION

Think about and/or discuss these questions:

1. Do parents arrange their children's marriages where you come from? Explain.
2. What happens to women in your country who do not marry?
3. How much control do you think parents should have over their adult children?
4. What does the word "liberal" mean to you? Do you consider yourself to be more liberal or more conservative? What about your parents? Explain.
5. What might be some reasons for a dowry system?
6. How have the roles of women changed in recent years? What do you think about these changes?

LIBRARY/INTERNET TASKS

Before you read the story:

1. Study a map of India and locate Bengal.
2. Find out about the dowry system in India.
3. Look up information on traditional Indian clothing, including saris.

Fasting, Feasting
Anita Desai

Anita Desai was born and educated in India. She now lives in the United States and teaches writing. We have selected an excerpt (short section) from her book *Fasting, Feasting.* Desai was a finalist for the British Booker Prize in 1999 with this book. In the book, Uma is the elder daughter of an Indian family. Her parents tried to arrange a marriage for her twice, but things did not work out. So Uma stays home and lives a very boring life taking care of her parents, who do not understand her.

The bold words should be learned. The numbered words are explained to help you understand the story. Some words have more than one meaning. The meaning we give is the closest synonym.

warning:
words that tell you
something bad will happen

Mama screwed up[1] her eyes and got to her feet. Staring into the morning glare[2], she finally said, in a **warning** voice, 'There's Dr Dutt coming.'

1 screwed up:
almost closed, squinted

2 glare: bright light

3 bundling away: putting away

4 mending: sewing

5 grunted: made sounds in a low, rough voice

6 irritably: angrily

7 aberration: different or not normal situation

8 dismounted: got off

9 unhitched the tuck: opened the fold

10 sari: female Indian clothing

11 no-nonsense: sensible, practical

12 throwing in: adding

13 humming: singing with closed lips

14 scattered: spread

15 reprimand: criticism

16 slopping over: spilling

17 batch: group

18 Institute: society, organization

19 matron (British): nurse in charge

20 masking: hiding

21 lack of interest: absence of curiosity

22 wound up: finished speaking

23 sloshed out: fell out, spilled

24 in agitation: upset

'Dr Dutt? cried Uma, **instantly** bundling away[3] the mending[4] she had been given to do and preparing to enjoy the visit.

'Unf,' Papa grunted[5] irritably[6], although he was doing nothing at all that she might **interrupt**. He did not say anything—Dr Dutt's father had been the Chief Justice at one time, it was a **distinguished** family, and if the daughter was still unmarried at fifty, and a working woman as well, it was an aberration[7] he had to **tolerate**. In fact, Papa was quite **capable of** putting on a **progressive, westernized front** when **called upon** to do so—in public, in society, not within his family, of course—and now he showed his **liberal**, educated ways by rising to his feet when Dr Dutt dismounted[8] from her bicycle, unhitched the tuck[9] she had made in her sari[10] to keep it out of the bicycle chain's teeth, and came up the steps with her quick, no-nonsense[11] walk.

Uma was sent to make lemonade for Dr Dutt. She did so **enthusiastically** throwing in[12] an extra spoon of sugar and humming[13] even when most of it scattered[14] over the kitchen table, bringing forth an angry reprimand[15] from the cook who would be the one who had to explain where all that sugar went, as he reminded her. Uma laughed at him and went out with the lemonade slopping over[16] the **tray** because pleasure made her steps **uneven**. She had last seen Dr Dutt at the Christmas bazaar when she had bought a packet of cards at Uma's stall.

◉ Who was happy to see Dr Dutt? Who was not?
◉ Why does Papa really disapprove of Dr Dutt?
◉ How does he behave towards her?

'—and this new batch[17] of nurses is already **installed** in the new **dormitory**, twenty-two of them, and the Institute[18] has only just realized that it did not **employ** a matron[19] or a housekeeper to run it for them,' Dr Dutt was telling MamaPapa who sat side by side on the swing and listened with **identical** expressions masking[20] their lack of interest[21]. Why was she telling them about the nurses' dormitory, the Medical Institute, the **arrangements** made or not made there? Such talk was neither about their family nor their circle of friends—how could it interest them?

Dr Dutt nodded at Uma as she saw her come out with the tray of lemonade. 'And so I thought of Uma,' Dr Dutt wound up[22]. Uma nearly dropped the tray and **steadied** only after half the lemonade had sloshed out[23] onto it.

Mama sat up in agitation[24]. 'Tchh! Look what you have done. What will Dr Dutt think of you? Go and get another glass.'

instantly: at once, immediately

interrupt: stop

distinguished: successful and respected

tolerate: accept

capable of: able to

progressive: modern

westernized front: European or North American behavior

called upon: required

liberal: open-minded

enthusiastically: excitedly

tray: like a plate, only bigger and used for carrying food/drinks

uneven: not regular or balanced

installed: living, settled

dormitory: building where many people sleep

employ: hire

identical: exactly the same

arrangements: plans

steadied: got balanced

dripping: wet

'No, no, no,' Dr Dutt cried and took the half-filled and **dripping** glass. "I came to see Uma and talk to Uma. And I can't stay long. The beginning of term is a very busy time for us, you see. So we really need Uma to come and help us.'

'Help?' Uma gulped[25], awkwardly[26] sitting down beside Dr Dutt who put her hand on her arm. Dr Dutt's hold was firm. 'Help?'

'Didn't you hear? Didn't you hear what Dr Dutt was saying?' Papa asked irritably.

sequence of events: series of happenings

'No,' said Uma and Dr Dutt again rattled through[27] the **sequence of events** that had left the Medical Institute with a new dormitory and new nurses and no one to take care of them while they were in training.

'So, you see, I thought of you, Uma. A young woman with no employment, who has been running the house for her parents for so long. I feel sure you would be right for the job.'

novel: new

'Job?' gulped Uma, never having aspired[28] so high in her life, and found the idea as **novel** as that of being **launched into space**.

launched into space: sent to outer space

Papa looked incredulous[29] and Mama outraged[30]. Dr Dutt still clasped Uma's arm. 'Don't look so frightened,' she urged. 'I know how well you looked after your parents. I know how much you helped Mrs. O'Henry with her work. I am **confident** you can do it.

confident: sure

But Uma was not confident. 'I have no degree,' she faltered[31], 'or training.'

assured: promised

authorities: people in charge

adored: loved

'This kind of work does not require training, Uma,' Dr Dutt **assured** her, or degrees. Just leave that to me. I will deal with it if the **authorities** ask. You will agree, sir?' she turned to Papa, smiling, as if she knew how much he **adored** being called sir.

◉ What was Dr Dutt's reason for visiting? What does she offer Uma?
◉ What does Uma think about the offer?
◉ What do Uma's parents think about the offer?

honour (British spelling): respect

frown: angry look

step into: enter

occupied: lived in

But Papa did not appear to have noticed the **honour** this time. He was locking his face up into a **frown** of great degree[32]. The frown was filled with everything he thought of working women, of women who dared presume[33] to **step into** the world he **occupied**. Uma knew that and cringed[34].

'Papa,' she said pleadingly[35].

provide for: support

It was Mama who spoke, however. As usual, for Papa. Very clearly and decisively[36]. 'Our daughter does not need to go out to work, Dr Dutt.' she said. 'As long as we are here to **provide for** her, she will never need to work.'

25 gulped: swallowed hard

26 awkwardly: uncomfortably

27 rattled through: spoke about

28 aspired: thought, dreamed

29 incredulous: unable or unwilling to believe

30 outraged: angry and shocked

31 faltered: said weakly

32 degree: size

33 dared presume: believed they had the right

34 cringed: felt embarrassed

35 pleadingly: anxiously, desperately

36 decisively: with certainty

'But she works all the time!' Dr Dutt **exclaimed** on a rather sharp note[37]. 'At home. Now you must give her a chance to work outside—'

'There is no need,' Papa supported Mama's view. In double strength[38] it grew formidable[39]. 'Where is the need?'

Dr Dutt persisted[40]. 'Shouldn't we ask Uma for her view? Perhaps she would like to go out and work? After all, it is at my own Institute, in a women's dormitory, with other women. I can vouch for[41] the **conditions**, they are perfectly **decent**, sir. You may come and **inspect** the dormitory, meet the nurses, see for yourself. Would you like to pay us a visit, Uma?

Uma bobbed[42] her head **rapidly** up and down. She worked hard at **controlling her expression**; she knew her face was twitching[43] in every direction. She knew her parents were watching. She tried to say yes, please, yes please, yespleaseyes—

'Go and take the tray away,' Mama said.

Uma's head was bobbing, her lips were fluttering[44]: yes, yespleaseyes.

'Uma,' Mama repeated, and her voice brought Uma to her feet. She took up the tray and went into the kitchen. She stood there, wrapping her hands into her sari, saying into the corner behind the icebox: pleasepleaseplease—

Then she went back to the verandah[45]—warily[46], warily. Dr Dutt was sitting very **upright** in her basket chair. She looked directly at Uma. 'I am very sorry,' she said 'I am very sorry to hear that.'

◉ What does Papa think about women who go out to work?
◉ According to Mama, why doesn't Uma need to go out to work?
◉ What does Uma want?

Hear what? What?

Mama was getting to her feet. She walked Dr Dutt down the verandah steps to her waiting bicycle. 'Isn't it difficult to **cycle** in a sari?' she asked with a little laugh, and looked pointedly[47] at the frayed[48] and oily[49] hem[50] of Dr Dutt's sari.

Dr Dutt did not answer but tucked it up[51] at her waist and stood steadying the bicycle. She did not look back at Uma but Uma heard her say to Mama, 'If you have that problem, you must come to the hospital for tests. If you need the hysterectomy[52], it is better to get it done soon. There is no need to live like an invalid[53]. She mounted the small, hard leather seat and bicycled away, the wheels crushing the gravel[54] and making it spurt up[55] in a reddish **spray**.

Uma stopped twitching her hands in a fold of her sari and looked towards Mama. Hysterectomy—what was that?

squeeze: press firmly

Mama came up the steps and linked arms[56] with Uma, giving her an affectionate[57] little **squeeze**. 'And so my madcap[58] wanted to run away and leave her Mama? What will my madcap do next?'

❀　　❀　　❀

The next time MamaPapa went to the club and Uma was alone in the house, she slipped into[59] Papa's office room. The phone that had once stood on a three-legged table in the drawing room[60] and then moved to his desk was now locked in a wooden box, but Uma knew where he kept the key. She scrabbled around[61] in the inky pencil box and found it amongst defunct[62] pens and split nibs[63], unlocked the box

dialed: rang

guilty:
in the wrong, at fault

disturbing: interrupting

and quickly **dialed** Dr Dutt's number. It was Dr Dutt's residential[64] number and she felt **guilty** about **disturbing** the doctor at home on a Sunday evening. But it was an emergency, of a kind.

Dr Dutt did sound a little unhappy at being disturbed. 'Yes, Uma dear,' she sighed, 'I wish your parents had agreed but what could I say when your mother told me she was not well and needs you to nurse her?'

'Dr Dutt,' Uma cried, 'Mama is not ill. She's not!'

There was a moment's silence. Was Dr Dutt thinking over the situation or was she brushing one of her pet dogs, or drinking from a cup

luxury: great comfort

solitude: privacy

passionately:
greatly, with much feeling

of tea? What did Dr Dutt do in the **luxury** of her **solitude**? Uma stood on one leg and wished **passionately** that she knew.

❀ Why does Mama say she needs Uma?

❀ Do you think Mama is telling the truth? Or is it an excuse?

❀ What does Uma do when her parents leave the house?

Finally Dr Dutt's voice emerged[65], guarded[66], 'I don't know about that—we'll find out when she comes for her tests.'

'She won't, Dr Dutt, she won't. I know it. Mama's all right! I know she is. You can ask Papa—'

'Your mother may not like that, Uma.'

Uma clenched her teeth[67] so as not to let out a wail[68] of anger and

protest:
objection, complaint

protest that welled up[69] in her mouth like blood when a tooth is drawn[70]. 'Then tell her to come for the tests,' she begged. 'Phone Mama and tell her to come. You will see, she won't.'

Dr Dutt tried to placate[71] Uma. 'Let's wait till she comes, and then we'll see what is wrong. If it turns out nothing's wrong, perhaps we can talk about the job again.'

'But will the job still be there? If the Institute gets someone else— then? Couldn't you tell Mama to be quick so I can get the job?'

Dr Dutt sighed. 'All right. Call her to the phone and I will speak to her.'

'She is out now,' Uma had to admit.

56 linked arms: joined arms

57 affectionate:
friendly, warm

58 madcap: foolish child

59 slipped into:
went quietly into

60 drawing room (British):
living room

61 scrabbled around:
looked, searched

62 defunct: useless

63 nibs: writing tips of pens

64 residential: home

65 emerged: came out

66 guarded: careful

67 clenched her teeth:
closed her jaw tightly

68 wail: cry

69 welled up:
rose up, came up

70 drawn: pulled out

71 placate: calm down

72 dowry:
   marriage money paid to
   the husband's family

73 I'm ruined:
   I have no money left

74 pauper: very poor person

'Oh,' Dr Dutt seemed to put something down heavily—or perhaps there was someone else in the room who did. 'I will telephone her later,' she promised, and rang off.

She did, next day, but Mama did not tell Uma what was said between them, and Uma could not ask. Uma was in **disgrace**: she had forgotten to lock up the telephone in its box and Papa had returned from the club to find the **evidence** of her **crime** staring at him from his office desk.

disgrace: trouble

evidence: signs

crime: bad action

'Costs money! Costs money!' he kept shouting, long after. 'Never earned anything in her life, made me spend and spend, on her dowry[72] and her wedding. Oh, yes, spend till I'm ruined[73], till I am a pauper[74]—'

⊚ Why does Uma phone Dr Dutt? What does the doctor tell her?
⊚ Why is Uma in disgrace?
⊚ What is Papa talking about at the end of the passage? Is it Uma's dowry and wedding?

EXPLORING THE STORY

AN ACTIVITY FOR GROUP DISCUSSION, HOMEWORK, OR YOUR JOURNAL

A good writer will not only describe interesting characters and an interesting plot—what happens in the story—but will also provide extra ideas or opinions that are not always easy to see.

Answer the activities and questions below. Always go back to the story to explain your answers.

1. The parents in this story are called Mama and Papa, and sometimes MamaPapa. What does it tell you about how Uma sees them?
   Do they treat Uma as a child or as an adult? Does Uma respond to them as a child or as an adult?

2. The writer uses descriptive words to show how Uma feels during Dr Dutt's visit. Write down five words and/or phrases that tell you how she feels happy to see her and how she feels nervous about the job.

3. The characters in this story are not honest about their true opinions, feelings, or actions. Next to each character's name, write examples of their dishonesty.
   Mama _____
   Papa _____
   Uma _____
   Dr Dutt _____

4. The main point of this story is:

  Parents have a right to keep their adult daughter at home

  Weak people can't be helped

  It isn't a good idea to try and help someone change his or her life

  Controlling parents can damage their children's future

5. What would be a good title for this story?

EXPLORING THE VOCABULARY

Complete the following sentences with bold words from the story. Change the form of the word when necessary.

1. The police found _____ of the crime—fingerprints.

2. The police decided to _____ the homes of the thieves.

3. I _____ that I had been out of the country at the time.

4. If they arrested me it would be a _____.

5. I was _____ that if they compared fingerprints, I would be freed.

6. The _____ had to let me go.

7. The _____ of events was most unpleasant.

Now choose ten of the numbered words and write a sentence for each one. You may copy sentences from your dictionary.

EXPLORING THE LANGUAGE

LANGUAGE CHUNKS

Many students like to learn fixed expressions (words that usually go together) and then use these "chunks" of language in speaking or writing. This kind of learning is very common when you learn your first language. We recommend that you learn these language chunks.

Here is a list of chunks from "Fasting, Feasting." Study them. They are explained in the margins of the story.

sequence of events	launched into space
lack of interest	wound up
sloshed out	rattled through
step into	double strength
vouch for	tucked up

spurt up
slipped into
of a kind
welled up

linked arms
scrabbled around
clenched her teeth

Now complete these sentences with one of the expressions, changing the form of the words when necessary.

1. The Russians were the first to _____ a man _____.

2. The doctor said, "Please _____ my office and take a seat."

3. When the dentist pulled out my tooth, tears _____ in my eyes.

4. The novel did not sell well due to a _____.

5. When you order coffee, do you always ask for _____?

6. I carried my coffee out. I slipped and nearly fell and most of the coffee _____.

7. Most modern watches don't need to be _____ every day.

8. The two friends _____ and walked to school.

9. I _____ the kitchen at midnight and found something to eat.

10. Yes, she used to work for me. I can _____ her.

E X P L O R I N G   T H E   W R I T I N G

POETIC LICENSE

Writers do not always follow the rules of grammar or punctuation. They break these rules on purpose to communicate better with the reader. This is called poetic license. For example, in this story, the author breaks the rules when she writes "MamaPapa" as if the two persons were only one person with the exact same ideas and attitudes. It helps us understand why Uma finds this double opposition too strong to resist.

"She tried to say yes, please, yes please, yespleaseyes—" is another example of poetic license. Here the writer does not use commas or spaces between words. What effect does it have on you, the reader?

EXPLORING YOUR IDEAS

An Activity For Group Discussion, Homework, Or Your Journal

Read these sentences from the story and respond with your ideas and feelings. Discuss or write as much as possible because, as you do, more ideas will come to you.

1. Papa was quite capable of putting on a progressive, westernized front when called upon to do so—in public, in society. Not within his family, of course.
2. She tried to say yes, please, yes please, yespleaseyes—
3. But it was an emergency of a kind.
4. What did Dr Dutt do in the luxury of her solitude?
5. Uma was in disgrace.

EXPLORING THE INTERNET

Find information on the dowry system at **www.islamicvoice.com** and **www.christianitytoday.com** (enter "dowry" in the search fields).

Discover articles and information on people who are working towards dynamic change in Indian society at **www.indianest.com/society**.

SAFE (Save a Female through Education) helps educate female children in India. Read more about the organization and its work at **www.cse.nd.edu/~surendar/safe**.

For real stories of women who have started their own businesses in India, see **www.rd-india.com/entwom.htm**.

There are many organizations aimed at helping women become employed in India. One of them is SEWA (Self Employed Women's Association) at **www.sewa.org**. Don't miss the gallery link featuring beautiful photographs of women working in India.

We encourage you to do your own Internet search and share the sites you find with your classmates and with your teacher.

FOLLOW-UP ACTIVITIES

Choose one or more of the following activities to complete:

1. Imagine you are Uma and write a journal entry about Dr Dutt's visit or about your phone call to her.
2. Retell the story as though you were Mama or Papa.

3. Interview a woman who works outside the home. You can make an audio or a video tape or make a presentation to your class. Ask her the following questions and one or more questions of your own:
   What training did you get before you started working?
   What is the most enjoyable part of your work?
   What is your professional goal?
   Would you prefer not to work? Why or why not?

4. If Uma were your friend, how would you advise and support her? Write a letter or act out a dialogue with a classmate.

5. Paint, draw, or take a photograph to illustrate a scene from this story. Explain why you chose that particular scene.

6. Who do you agree with, Uma or her parents? Present your case in writing or orally.

7. Write a letter to a newspaper or an email to a newsgroup in which you complain about young people and their liberal ideas.

8. Find information on the dowry system in different cultures and present your information as part of a panel or in a report.

If you enjoyed reading this excerpt from Anita Desai's novel, we suggest that you read the whole book *Fasting, Feasting*. See the acknowledgements page for publishing information.

Unit
7

POOR VISITOR
Jamaica Kincaid

Antigua
and the USA

It was not my first bout with the disappointment of reality and it would not be my last.

Unit
7

POOR VISITOR
Jamaica Kincaid

Antigua
and the USA

INTRODUCTION

Think about and/or discuss these questions:

1. Do you know anyone who moved to a new country? What sort of changes did they expect? What surprised them?
2. Why do people move to another country? Name some of the reasons.
3. Have you or anyone you know been homesick? Explain.
4. What foreign place do you dream of visiting? Why is it interesting to you?

LIBRARY/INTERNET TASKS

Before you read the story:

1. Find information on the history and climate of Antigua.
2. Look for information on New York City's weather and main sights.

Poor Visitor

Jamaica Kincaid

Jamaica Kincaid was born in St. Johns, Antigua, an island in the Caribbean Sea. This excerpt (short selection) comes from the first chapter of her autobiographical novel, *Lucy.* It is about Lucy's experiences the first time she leaves her home to go and live in New York City. It describes the conflict between the dream that brings Lucy to New York and the reality she finds there. Lucy leaves Antigua and her family with high hopes for a different and happier life. But when she arrives in New York City, she has several problems "with the disappointment of reality."

The bold words should be learned. The numbered words are explained to help you understand the story. Some words have more than one meaning. The meaning we give is the closest synonym.

It was my first day. I had come the night before, a gray-black and cold night before—as it was expected to be in the middle of January, though I didn't know that at the time—and I could not see anything clearly on the way in from the airport, even though there were lights everywhere. As we drove along, someone would single out[1] to me a famous building, an important street, a park, a bridge that when built was thought to be a spectacle[2]. In a daydream I used to have, all these places were

1 single out:
choose something
special, point out

2 spectacle:
something special

3 lifeboats:
   boats sent to help
   people in danger

4 drowning:
   dying from being under
   water too long

5 soul:
   center of the
   heart and mind

6 fixture of fantasy:
   regular dream

7 bout: short difficult time

8 undergarments:
   underwear, clothes worn
   under other clothes

9 soundly: deeply

10 curl: turn up

11 madras: striped cotton

12 realization:
   understanding

points of happiness to me; all these places were lifeboats[3] to my small drowning[4] soul[5], for I would imagine myself entering and leaving them, and just that—entering and leaving over and over again—would see me through a bad feeling I did not have a name for. I only knew it felt like sadness. Now that I saw these places, they looked ordinary, dirty, worn down by so many people entering and leaving them in real life, and **it occurred to me** that I could not be the only person in the world for whom they were a fixture of fantasy[6]. It was not my first bout[7] with the disappointment of **reality** and it would not be my last. The undergarments[8] that I wore were all new, bought for my journey, and as I sat in the car, **twisting** this way and that to get a good view of the sights before me, I was reminded of how uncomfortable the new can make you feel.

I got into an **elevator**, something I had never done before, and then I was in an apartment and seated at a table, eating food just taken from a refrigerator. In Antigua, where I came from, I had always lived in a house, and my house did not have a refrigerator in it. Everything I was **experiencing**—the ride in the elevator, being in an apartment, eating day-old food that had been **stored** in a refrigerator—was such a good idea that I could imagine I would grow used to it and like it very much, but at first it was all so new that I had to smile with my mouth turned down at the corners. I slept soundly[9] that night, but it wasn't because I was happy and comfortable—quite the opposite; it was because I didn't want to take in anything else.

That morning, the morning of my first day, the morning that followed my first night, was a sunny morning. It was not the sort of bright sun-yellow making everything curl[10] at the edges, almost in fright, that I was used to, but a pale-yellow sun, as if the sun had grown weak from trying too hard to shine; but still it was sunny, and that was nice and made me miss my home less. And so, seeing the sun, I got up and put on a dress made out of madras[11] cloth—the same sort of dress that I would wear if I were at home and setting out for a day in the country. It was all wrong. The sun was shining but the air was cold. It was the middle of January, after all. But I did not know that the sun could shine and the air remain cold; no one had ever told me. What a feeling that was! How can I explain? Something I had always known—the way I knew my skin was the color of a nut rubbed repeatedly with a soft cloth, or the way I knew my own name—something I **took** completely **for granted**, "the sun is shining, the air is warm," was not so. I was no longer in a **tropical zone**, and this realization[12] now entered my life like a flow of water dividing formerly dry and **solid** ground, creating two banks, one of which was my past—so **familiar** and

it occurred to me:
I suddenly thought

reality:
the world of experience,
not imagination

twisting: turning

elevator:
machine that lifts people
from floor to floor

experiencing:
doing and feeling

stored: kept

took for granted:
believed to be certain

tropical zone:
hot area of the world

solid: firm, hard

familiar: easy to recognize

predictable: expected

blank: empty space

predictable that even my unhappiness then made me happy just to think of it—the other my future, a gray **blank**, an overcast[13] seascape[14] on which rain was falling, and no boats were in sight. I was no longer in a tropical zone and I felt cold inside and out, the first time such a sensation[15] had come over me.

⚹ What places does Lucy describe upon arriving in New York? How had she imagined them?
⚹ Name three new experiences in her new place.
⚹ Why does she sleep soundly the first night?
⚹ What surprising thing does she learn the next morning?

homesickness: missing home

situation: place, condition

impatient: angry, annoyed

In books I had read—from time to time, when the plot called for it—someone would suffer from **homesickness**. A person would leave a not very nice **situation** and go somewhere else, somewhere a lot better, and then long to go back where it was not very nice. How **impatient** I would become with such a person, for I would feel that I was in a not very nice situation myself, and how I wanted to go somewhere else. But now I, too, felt that I wanted to be back where I came from. I understood it, I knew where I stood there. If I had to draw a picture of my future then, it would have been a large gray patch[16], surrounded by black, blacker, blackest.

13 overcast: cloudy, not clear

14 seascape: view of the sea

15 sensation: feeling

16 patch: area

gesture: movement of the body

in general: as a whole

What a surprise this was to me, that I longed to be back in the place that I came from, that I longed to sleep in a bed I had outgrown[17], that I longed to be with people whose smallest, most natural **gesture** would call up in me such a rage[18] that I longed to see them dead at my feet. Oh, I had imagined that with one swift[19] act—leaving home and coming to this new place—I could leave behind me, as if it were an old garment[20] never to be worn again, my sad thoughts, my sad feelings, and my discontent[21] with life **in general** as it presented[22] itself to me. In the past, the thought of being in my present situation had been a comfort, but now I did not even have this to look forward to, and so I lay down on my bed and dreamt that I was eating a bowl of pink mullet[23] and green figs[24] cooked in coconut milk, and it had been cooked by my grandmother, which was why the taste of it pleased me so, for she was the person I liked best in all the world and those were the things I liked best to eat also.

The room in which I lay was a small room just off the kitchen—the maid's room. I was used to a small room, but this was a different sort of small room. The ceiling was very high and the walls went all the way up to the ceiling, enclosing[25] the room like a box—a box in which cargo[26]

17 I had outgrown: too small for me

18 rage: strong anger

19 swift: quick

20 garment: piece of clothing

21 discontent: unhappiness

22 presented: showed, appeared

23 mullet: fish

24 figs: fruit that grows in warm climates

25 enclosing: surrounding

26 cargo: things sent by air, sea, or ground

traveling a long way should be shipped. But I was not cargo. I was only an unhappy young woman living in a maid's room, and I was not even the maid. I was the young girl who watches over the children and goes to school at night. How nice everyone was to me, though, saying that I should **regard** them as my family and make myself at home. I believed them to be **sincere**, for I knew that such a thing would not be said to a member of their real family. After all, aren't family the people who become the millstone around your life's neck[27]? On the last day I spent at home, my cousin—a girl I had known all my life, an unpleasant person even before her parents forced her to become a Seventh-Day Adventist[28]—made a farewell[29] present to me of her own Bible, and with it she made a little speech about God and goodness and blessings. Now it sat before me on a dresser[30], and I remembered how when we were children we would sit under my house and torment[31] each other by reading out loud passages from the Book of Revelations[32], and I wondered if ever in my whole life a day would go by when these people I had left behind, my own family, would not appear before me in one way or another.

regard: think of
sincere: honest

✕ How does Lucy feel about the present?
✕ How does she see her future?
✕ What surprising feelings does she have about her family?
✕ What are Lucy's duties in her new home?

There was also a small radio on this dresser, and I had turned it on. At that moment, almost as if to **sum up** how I was feeling, a song came on some of the words of which were "Put yourself in my place, if only for a day; see if you can stand the awful emptiness inside." I sang these words to myself over and over, as if they were a lullaby[33], and I fell asleep again. This time I dreamt that I was holding in my hands one of my old cotton-flannel **nightgowns**, and it was printed with beautiful scenes of children playing with Christmas-tree **decorations**. The scenes printed on my nightgown were so real that I could actually hear the children laughing. I felt compelled[34] to know where this nightgown came from, and I started to examine it furiously[35], looking for the label. I found it just where a label usually is, in the back, and it read "Made in Australia." I was awakened from this dream by the actual maid, a woman who had let me know right away, on meeting me, that she did not like me, and gave as her reason the way I talked. I thought it was because of something else, but I did not know what. As I opened my eyes, the word "Australia" stood between our faces, and I remembered then that Australia was settled as a prison for bad people, people so bad that they couldn't be put in a prison in their own country.

sum up: say in a few words

nightgowns:
dresses that women
wear to bed

decorations:
shiny pretty balls

routine: regular schedule

My waking hours soon took on a **routine**. I walked four small girls to their school, and when they returned at midday I gave them a lunch of soup from a tin, and sandwiches. In the afternoon, I read to them and played with them. When they were away, I studied my books, and at night I went to school. I was unhappy. I looked at a map. The Atlantic Ocean stood between me and the place I came from, but would it have made a difference if it had been a teacup of water? I could not go back.

Outside, it was cold, and everyone said it was the coldest winter they had ever experienced but the way they said it made me think they said this every time winter came around. And I couldn't **blame them for** not remembering each year how unpleasant, how unfriendly winter weather could be. The trees with their **bare**, still **limbs** looked dead, and as if someone had just placed them there and planned to come back and get them later; all the windows of the houses were shut tight, the way windows are shut up when a house will be empty for a long time; when people walked on the streets they did it quickly, as if they were doing something **behind someone's back**, as if they didn't want to draw attention to themselves, as if being out in the cold too long would cause them to **dissolve**. How I longed to see someone lingering[36] on a corner, trying to **draw** my **attention** to him, trying to **engage me in conversation**, someone complaining to himself in a voice I could overhear about a god whose love and mercy[37] fell on the just[38] and the unjust.

I wrote home to say how lovely everything was, and I used flourishing[39] words and phrases, as if I were living life in a **greeting card**—the kind that has a satin ribbon on it, and quilted[40] hearts and roses, and is expected to be so **precious** to the person receiving it that the **manufacturer** has placed a leaf[41] of plastic on the front to protect it. Everyone I wrote to said how nice it was to hear from me, how nice it was to know that I was doing well, that I was very much missed, and that they couldn't wait until the day came when I returned.

✻ Who doesn't like Lucy? Why?
✻ Why doesn't Lucy like New York City in the winter? What does she miss about Antigua?
✻ What kind of letters does she send and receive?

blame them for: say they were wrong for

bare: without leaves, naked

limbs: branches

behind someone's back: in secret

dissolve: make something solid become liquid

draw attention: have people look at them

engage me in conversation: speak to me

greeting card: card for a special occasion

precious: valuable

manufacturer: company that makes things

36 lingering: waiting

37 mercy: pity

38 just: good

39 flourishing: elegant, fancy

40 quilted: thick cloth

41 leaf: sheet

EXPLORING THE STORY

AN ACTIVITY FOR GROUP DISCUSSION, HOMEWORK, OR YOUR JOURNAL

A good writer will not only describe interesting characters and an interesting plot—what happens in the story—but will also provide extra ideas or opinions that are not always easy to see.

Answer the activities and questions below. Always go back to the story to explain your answers.

1. Complete the following grid with words from the text, telling what Lucy knew or imagined about New York City while she was still in Antigua, and what she discovered once she moved to New York. The first one is done for you.

Themes	Antigua	New York
special places	points of happiness, lifeboats	ordinary, dirty, worn
housing		
food		
climate		
clothing		
family		
people outside		
Lucy's feelings		

2. Using the information you wrote down in the grid above, write a short paragraph explaining how Lucy feels and why.

3. The following grid contains a list of words the author uses to describe Lucy's feelings and the world outside. Put an X in the appropriate column that the word describes. The first one is done for you.

Author's Words	Lucy's Feelings	World Outside
bare		x
black		
blackest		
cold		
coldest		
dead		
dirty		
emptiness		
gray		
ordinary		
overcast		
rain		
unfriendly		
unhappy		
unpleasant		
winter		
worn		

4. Count how many times the word "cold" or one of its forms is used. Why does the author use the word "cold" so often? What effect does it have on you, the reader?

5. What can you say about Lucy's inner and outer worlds?

6. On page 79, read aloud the paragraph that begins with, "That morning…" and read up to "How can I explain?" What word is repeated several times throughout the section? Substitute the word with the word "it" where you can and read the passage aloud again. What differences, if any, do you hear? Which version do you prefer? Why?

7. Choose the word that best describes Lucy's feelings in the paragraph you just read. Use your dictionary if you don't know a word: astonishment, surprise, interest, amazement, wonder. Explain your choice.

8. Jamaica Kincaid also uses "sound devices." This is an example from the first paragraph in which the sounds /s/ and /z/ and /th/ are repeated, giving the impression of a sigh:

   "…all these places were points of happiness to me; all these places were lifeboats to my small drowning soul…"

9. Look at the three sentences below. Read them aloud and underline the sounds that are repeated:

   "…my sad thoughts, my sad feelings, and my discontent with life in general as it presented itself to me."

   "…I should regard them as my family and make myself at home."

   "…quilted hearts and roses, and is expected to be so precious to the person receiving it that the manufacturer has placed a leaf of plastic on the front to protect it."

EXPLORING THE VOCABULARY

Complete the following sentences with bold words from the story. Change the form of the word when necessary.

1. You failed the test because you didn't study. Don't
   _____ the teacher.

2. They always talked about him _____ his

   _____ .

3. You need to go and see the dentist. Don't worry. It's just a
   _____ check-up.

4. I don't like this _____ . It's dangerous. We need to get out of here.

5. Yes, you can believe her. She's a _____ friend.

6. I _____ Tom as an expert. He knows everything about chess.

7. When water freezes, it becomes _____ .

8. When you put sugar in hot tea or coffee it _____ .

9. Diamonds are _____ stones.

10. I thought we were lost, but now the area looks more

    _____ .

Now choose ten of the numbered words and write a sentence for each one. You may copy sentences from your dictionary.

EXPLORING THE LANGUAGE

LANGUAGE CHUNKS

Many students like to learn fixed expressions (words that usually go together) and then use these "chunks" of language in speaking or writing. This kind of learning is very common when you learn your first language. We recommend that you learn these language chunks.

Here is a list of chunks from "Poor Visitor." Study them. They are explained in the margins.

in general	millstone around your neck
occurred to	take for granted
single out	sum up
behind someone's back	draw attention
engage in conversation	greeting card

Now complete these sentences with one of the expressions, changing the form of the words when necessary.

1. In some countries people send _____ at special times like Christmas or New Year's.

2. She is a very social woman. Even if people are strangers to each other, she will _____ them _____.

3. Sometimes little children _____ to people who are different. "Look at that funny man!"

4. We have a job opening and it _____ me that you might be interested.

5. _____, I believe that parents shouldn't do anything for their children that children can do for themselves.

6. She thought he had _____ her _____ and danced with her all evening because he liked her. Sadly she realized later that he wanted to make someone else jealous.

7. To _____, you need to work much harder and come to work on time if you want to keep this job.

8. You have always _____ me _____. You don't care about me. You don't really love me. I'm leaving!

9. When I was young, I had to take my little brothers with me wherever I went. They were a _____.

10. Another worker in my department went _____ and told the boss that I came late every day. It's a lie.

EXPLORING THE WRITING

AUTOBIOGRAPHICAL WRITING

The word *biography* means a book or a story about another person's life. The author of the book is expected to be correct and complete about all the information in the book. The central character is usually referred to as "he" or "she."

An *autobiography* is a book or a story written by the author about himself or herself. It also needs to be correct in the information it gives the reader. The author often uses "I" in such a book, but may also use "he" or "she." *Lucy,* the book from which this story comes, is an *autobiographical novel.* This means that the main character in the book is the same person who wrote it. In this case, Jamaica Kincaid is both the author and the narrator—the person who tells the story in the book.

In an autobiographical novel, the author has more freedom in deciding what information to use than in an autobiography. Although the important facts are correct, the author can invent situations or people to make the story more interesting or easier to read. In this autobiographical novel, for example, the author chooses to give herself a different name, "Lucy." But the author really moved from Antigua to New York at a young age, and really lived with a family and looked after their children. The author may use "I," as in our story, or she might have used "she."

Other examples of autobiographical novels or stories in this book are Units 2, 3, and 10. For an explanation of "fiction" and "novel," go to the *Exploring the Writing* section in Unit 4.

EXPLORING YOUR IDEAS

Read these sentences from the story and respond with your ideas and feelings. Discuss or write as much as possible because, as you do, more ideas will come to you.

1. I was reminded of how uncomfortable the new can make you feel.
2. I felt cold inside and out, the first time such a sensation had come over me.
3. What a surprise this was to me, that I longed to be back in the place that I came from...
4. After all, aren't family the people who become the millstone around your neck?
5. I could not go back...
6. I wrote home to say how lovely everything was.

EXPLORING THE INTERNET

Explore Antigua online! For information on Antigua's culture and history, see **www.antigua-barbuda.org**. For beautiful pictures of the island of Antigua, visit the "Photo Album" at **www.turq.com/antigua/links.html**.

To view and download pictures of famous places in New York City, visit **www.atpm.com/6.10/new-york**.

You will find a biography of Jamaica Kincaid at **www.bbc.co.uk/worldservice/arts/features/womenwriters/ kincaid_life.shtml**. Click on the "being a woman writer" link to read interviews with Jamaica Kincaid and find interesting information on her work, writing style, and life events.

Discover more writers of the Caribbean at **personal.ecu.edu/deenas/caribbean/carbwtrs.htm**.

The "weekly voice" of the Caribbean-American community, **www.nycaribnews.com**, is an online version of this New York City-based newspaper. You'll find news, fashion, sports, and more!

We encourage you to do your own Internet search and share the sites you find with your classmates and with your teacher.

FOLLOW-UP ACTIVITIES

Choose one or more of the following activities to complete:

1. Have you ever been homesick? Write an entry in your journal describing how you felt at the time and what you did about it.
2. With a partner, write a phone conversation between Lucy and a friend still in Antigua in which Lucy tells her true feelings and the friend tries to comfort her. Act it out for the class.
3. Have you ever lived away from your family? Tell or write what was good or difficult about it.
4. What was your first job? How did your employer treat you? What did you learn from the experience? Share with a group or a partner.
5. Do you have a special song that expresses how you felt at one time? Share it with your classmates and explain what the song means to you.
6. Draw or paint a picture to illustrate this story. Share it with your classmates.
7. Write a recipe for your favorite food. Give it to someone in your class. Prepare the food and bring it to class.

8. Give a presentation about Antigua or another Caribbean island using maps, pictures, and other audiovisual aids. If possible, include music in your presentation.
9. Find out more about Jamaica Kincaid's "rags to riches" story. Write a short paper about her in the form of a newspaper article.

If you enjoyed reading this chapter from Jamaica Kincaid's novel, we suggest that you read the whole book, *Lucy*. See the acknowledgements page for publishing information.

Unit

8

ABOUT THE WEDDING FEAST
Ama Ata Aidoo

Ghana

It's the education. It takes away some very important part of understanding from them.

Unit
8

ABOUT THE WEDDING FEAST
Ama Ata Aidoo

Ghana

INTRODUCTION

Think about and/or discuss these questions:

1. Have you been to a wedding? Describe what happened, who was invited, and what foods were served.
2. Have you ever attended a wedding from a different culture? In what ways was it different from weddings in your culture?
3. How have wedding traditions changed since the time of your grandparents?
4. In general, who pays for the cost of the wedding in your culture?

LIBRARY/INTERNET TASKS

Before you read the story:

1. Find a map of Africa and locate the country of Ghana.
2. Find out what the climate is like and what types of food people eat in Ghana.

About the Wedding Feast
Ama Ata Aidoo

Ama Ata Aidoo has written plays, novels, poetry, and short stories. In 1982 she was appointed Minister of Education in Ghana and has since resigned. She is an educator who has lectured in Africa and the United States. This short story is from her book *The Girl Who Can and Other Stories.*

The bold words should be learned. The numbered words are explained to help you understand the story. Some words have more than one meaning. The meaning we give is the closest synonym.

announcement: news

It had begun with the **announcement** itself. That those two were going to get married. My granddaughter just came in from her workplace one early evening and told us. No asking. It was all telling. That was when something hit me. Yes, from that early. That there was something not right already. In the old days, when things were done **properly**, a girl did not just announce that sort of thing in that sort of way. But later, when I pointed that out[1] to the child's mother, my daughter Mary, she said that things have changed.

properly: correctly, well

1 pointed that out: said

2 *hei* (West African):
   exclamation

3 palm kernel:
   seed of the palm tree

4 coconut:
   large, brown nut
   from a palm tree;
   it has white flesh

5 intended: planned

6 hinting (West African):
   suggesting it to,
   indicating it to

7 handled: taken care of

8 grieve: be so sad

9 blessing:
   good luck, good fortune

10 finalize: decide

11 the slightest: any

12 proposed marriage:
   planned marriage

13 relieved: comforted

Hei[2], and how they have changed! And of course, being my daughter Mary, hard as a palm kernel[3] outside and coconut[4]-soft inside, she later came and without apologizing for speaking like that to me, asked me how the young lady should have informed us about what she and her young man intended[5]…

And then there was the matter of the time. How can a serious discussion like marriage intentions start at the end of the day? In the old days, if a young woman wanted to **bring up** such a matter, she would begin by just hinting[6] one of her mothers on her mother's side, who would hint her mother, and then I and her mother would have **discreetly** mentioned it to any other mothers and grandmothers whom we considered close enough to be brought into the discussion and the **negotiations** that would follow. Then, very early the next morning (at **dawn** really) we would have had a meeting, in my room certainly, sitting down properly, of course… But here I go again, forgetting that things have changed!

In this case, the young lady came to just tell us. And that was how everything got handled[7]. In the modern, educated way, and not at all properly.

Maybe, I should not have let myself grieve[8]: since for a start, we were in a **foreign land**. The young man my granddaughter was going to marry is from one part of Africa that is quite far from our country. My daughter Mary had sent me a ticket to go and visit her and her husband and children. Indeed, let me tell the truth: when it comes to such **gestures**, Mary is good. So I had gone. As everybody knows, this was the second or third time. In fact, I was preparing to return home here when the announcement came from my grandchild. That was a blessing[9]. Because, the way things have changed, I could sense that they were going to **go ahead** and finalize[10] everything, when no one at home had the slightest[11] knowledge about the proposed marriage[12]. And then, what was I going to tell everybody when I came back? You would all have **laughed at** me, no? That I too had gone and lost my head abroad; the way all these educated people seem to do when they travel **overseas**.

So I had said to Mary my daughter: "Mary, it is true that things have changed, but have they really changed that much?"

"Maybe not. Mother, … you only worry too much," was what she said. Now tell me, what kind of a response was that?

Anyway, that was when I came back here and informed you all about it. I had been quite surprised and very relieved[13] that you had such understanding. Was it you or Abanowa who had suggested that since the child was in a foreign land anyway, and the young man she was marrying does not come from anywhere around here, everybody

bring up: mention

discreetly: privately

negotiations: agreements

dawn:
first light of day, sunrise

foreign land:
another country

gestures: actions

go ahead: to move forward

laughed at:
to treat someone as if
they were stupid

overseas:
to a foreign country

question: possibility

background: family history

satisfactory: good enough

grateful: thankful

should accept that there was no **question** of anybody getting the chance to go and check his **background** to make sure everything about him and his family was **satisfactory**, and so if I found him acceptable, that should be fine with you all? At the time, I had not commented on it, but oh, I was so **grateful** for that.

As I had informed you all at the family meeting, I knew that Mary was going to be sending me a ticket to go back there for the wedding. But she had sent it much earlier… Mary doesn't know how to do a lot of things. In that she is not alone. It's the education. It takes away some very important part of understanding from them. But then, I must also say for Mary that those things she knows how to do, she does them very well.

So, that was how I came to be present at the big meeting between Mary and the boy's mother about what should be prepared for the **wedding feast**… To **tell the truth**, I had not really felt too happy at the idea of a joint[14] discussion. It was not right. What **self-respecting** family in the old days would ask for help from their prospective[15] in-laws? Whether it was in the way of just ideas or for something more substantial[16] like the actual preparation of food for the wedding feast? But when I so much as opened my mouth, Mary said these days, that is not only right, but even expected[17]. She added that in fact, she might hurt feelings if she didn't ask for the help. Mmm, things have really changed, haven't they?

Since there was not going to be any grandmother from the boy's side at the meeting, Mary and I agreed that even though I would sit in on the discussions I would keep a respectable silence. Which was what I did. However, every now and then, my daughter whispered questions to me to which I gave discreet answers. It had not seemed as if there was much disagreement about anything. They had discussed every-thing in a friendly way: the wedding cake itself; other cakes; biscuits and buns[18]; how to do the groundnuts and the other things for the guests to munch and crunch…

Groundnuts? Oh yes, they are everywhere! Except in most places they call them peanuts[19]!

□ How was marriage discussed in the past? And now?
□ Where is the marriage going to take place?
□ What is the big meeting about? Is this a new or an old tradition?

They had sat and talked for a long time, maybe for as much as half of the day, when they came to the food that called for real cooking. That was when things began to take time to decide. I had been thinking, and

wedding feast: special dinner

tell the truth: be honest

self-respecting: good and correct

14 joint: two-family

15 prospective: future, potential

16 substantial: important

17 expected: depended on

18 biscuits and buns (British): cookies and small cakes

19 peanuts: little round nuts that grow in the ground in pea-like shells

even told them, that if they did not stop for a little rest and get something to eat, something **nasty** was going to happen. But Mary said, and it was **plain** that the boy's mother agreed with her, that it was better to finish everything at one sitting[20]. I was going to open my mouth and tell them that since the beginning of creation[21], no family had finished planning what should go into a wedding feast at one sitting. But then I remembered that things have changed, and warned my lips[22].

Then it happened and I was not at all surprised. I had heard Mary mention *jolof*[23] and other dishes from our country. Then maybe, just for the shortest bit of time, I had got lost in my own thoughts and had not paid attention to the discussions. Because I had not noticed that something had **come up** which was really cutting their tempers short[24]. All I saw was suddenly, Mary and the boy's mother standing up at the same time and each of them **shouting**:

"That's no food, and you are not serving it at my daughter's wedding."

"That's no food, and you are not serving it at my son's wedding."

"Spinach stewed with a mixture of meat and fish?" shouted one with a sneer[25] that was big enough to wither[26] a virgin[27] forest.

"Spinach stewed only with onions and without meat or fish?" shouted the other, the **contempt** in her voice heavy enough to **crush a giant**.

"What do you mean?" shouted one.

"What do you mean?" countered[28] the other.

"I said that is no food, and you are not going to serve it at my child's wedding!" they both **screamed** at the same time.

"You cannot tell me that," one wailed[29].

"You cannot tell me that," the other whined[30] after her.

"Our guests will not eat that," one spat out[31].

"Our guests will laugh at us if you serve that," said the other.

"They will tell everyone in our community."

"They will write home to everybody in our country about it."

"It's awful, **a mess**."

"Yours is unclean."

"Yours is completely tasteless."

"But you ate it when you came to our house?" said one perplexed[32].

"But you ate it when you came to our house?" said the other, equally perplexed.

"No, I didn't, I didn't touch it," they both confessed[33].

"Eh?!"

"I went and threw it in the rubbish bin[34] in the kitchen."

"W-h-a-t?"

They made as if they were going to clutch[35] at each other's **throats**.

20 at one sitting:
    in one meeting

21 the beginning of creation:
    the beginning of time

22 warned my lips:
    told myself not to speak

23 *jolof* (West African):
    a spicy rice dish

24 cutting their
    tempers short:
    making them angry

25 sneer:
    smile without respect

26 wither:
    dry out, weaken

27 virgin: very old

28 countered: replied

29 wailed:
    said sadly and loudly

30 whined: said unhappily

31 spat out: said angrily

32 perplexed:
    confused, not
    understanding

33 confessed: admitted

34 rubbish bin (British):
    garbage can

35 clutch: grab, seize

nasty: bad, unpleasant

plain: clear

come up: happened

shouting: speaking loudly

contempt: lack of respect

crush a giant:
break an enormous person

screamed:
spoke loudly in a high voice

a mess: dirty

throats: necks

"Mother, mother, what is this?"

None of us who were already in the room had seen or felt my granddaughter and the young man come in. But they had.

"What is this?" they repeated. The mothers stopped dead. **Shame** on their faces, each stared at the boy and girl in the hallway[36]. For what had seemed a very long time, there was complete silence. Then the boy and the girl looked at one another, burst out[37] laughing, didn't say anything else to anybody and then went out of the room, still laughing.

What did the mothers do? What could they do? Each of them just sat down and stayed sat. And quiet. After some time, I called my daughter Mary's name.

"What is it?" she asked, glaring[38] at me.

"Listen," I said, my voice low. "I think you people had better stop now and continue with the planning of the feast tomorrow."

"What is there to plan?... Anyway, I am finished with all that," Mary said. And with that she went out of the room.

And that's how everything ended with the food affair. Oh yes, there was a wedding. And it was not only the ceremony[39] itself that went well. Everything else was wonderful. We cooked our *palaver sauce*[40] of spinach with *egusi*[41], meat and fish. The boy's people cooked their very plain spinach, without meat or fish... And did the guests eat? Don't even ask. They ate and ate and ate and ate. Since then, I have not heard that anyone from the boy's side **complained** about the food we cooked. And I am not hearing anyone from our side complain about the food our in-laws cooked...

You see oh...what still **puzzles** me is how people can tell others how much things have changed, when they do not prepare their own minds to handle such changes, eh...And as my mother used to say:

"What's food anyway? Once it goes down the throat..."

☐ Why do the mothers fight?
☐ What do the children do?
☐ Are there complaints after the wedding feast?

---

shame: embarrassment, guilt

complained: objected

puzzles: confuses

---

36 in the hallway: outside the door

37 burst out: suddenly began

38 glaring: looking angrily

39 ceremony: formal religious or legal event

40 *palaver sauce* (West African): stew (food cooked slowly in liquid)

41 *egusi* (West African): melon seeds eaten in West Africa

EXPLORING THE STORY

AN ACTIVITY FOR GROUP DISCUSSION, HOMEWORK, OR YOUR JOURNAL

A good writer will not only describe interesting characters and an interesting plot—what happens in the story—but will also provide extra ideas or opinions that are not always easy to see.

Read the questions below and think about them. Always go back to the story to explain your answers.

1. This story is written as a "monologue"—one person talking to an audience. Inside this monologue are "dialogues"—two or more persons talking to one another.
   a) Who is talking in the monologue? What is her position in the family? Who is her audience? How do you know?
   b) Who are the other people talking in this story? What are their positions in the family?

2. Write sentences about the narrator using these adjectives:
   sad _She is sad that things have changed so much._____

   surprised _____

   puzzled _____

   worried _____

   annoyed _____

   happy _____

   relieved _____

3. "About the Wedding Feast" is about the generational gap, that is, the differences in behavior and ideas between the grandmother, her daughter, and her granddaughter.
   a) Describe how a marriage was arranged when the grandmother was young. Who do you think "the mothers on her mother's side" are? Was the position of a grandmother more or less important? Explain.
   b) What changes in tradition does Mary accept? What is still important to her and why? What do the children think of their mothers' fight?

4. What does the narrator think of education? What is the difference between education and understanding? Do you agree or disagree with her? Explain your answer.

EXPLORING THE VOCABULARY

Complete the following sentences with bold words from the story. Change the form of the word when necessary.

1. When I became engaged to marry my husband in 1954, my family put an _____ in the newspaper.
2. Of course, they had checked his family _____ before they agreed to the marriage.
3. I was _____ that they approved of the match between us.
4. My father did _____ that my future husband was not as educated as I was.
5. It was _____ to me that my husband would work in the family business. He didn't need higher education.
6. I didn't realize that my education was considered a _____ by his grandparents.
7. They believed that my parents had not brought me up _____.
8. Very _____, his grandmother advised me to behave like an uneducated girl.
9. At that time, I did not even _____ her advice.
10. Today I tell my granddaughters that any _____ young woman needs the best education she can get so that she can take care of her family if she needs to do so.

Now choose ten of the numbered words and write a sentence for each one. You may copy sentences from your dictionary.

EXPLORING THE LANGUAGE

LANGUAGE CHUNKS

Many students like to learn fixed expressions (words that usually go together) and then use these "chunks" of language in speaking or writing. This kind of learning is very common when you learn your first language. We recommend that you learn these language chunks.

Here is a list of chunks from "About The Wedding Feast." Study them. They are explained in the margins of the story.

pointed out	come up
rubbish bin	at one sitting
spat out	burst out
wedding feast	tell the truth

laugh at   foreign land
go ahead   proposed marriage
bring up

Now complete these sentences with one of the expressions, changing the form of the words when necessary.

1. The subject hasn't _____ yet. But when it does, I'll tell Ada about it.
2. Chitty comes from a _____ and he doesn't know how to behave the way we do.
3. The _____ will not take place if I have any say. I don't trust him with her.
4. We _____ it _____ to them that we could pay for some of the wedding arrangements, but they wanted to pay for everything.
5. I told them to _____ and make all the arrangements. Someone would pay.
6. To _____, I really don't enjoy going to a wedding. It can be stressful!
7. I'm afraid that the little children will _____ laughing when they see their brother all dressed up in a tuxedo.
8. The little ones will also _____ Mary in her wedding dress.
9. They _____ words of hate to each other.
10. We arranged the wedding plans _____ because everyone was in a hurry to leave.

EXPLORING THE WRITING

VARIETIES OF ENGLISH

Because English is an international language, it has developed to represent all of its speakers all around the world. In Unit 2, we wrote about British and American English, which form two large older groups; however, there are many other groups with their own variations: Indian English, Singapore English, South African English, Caribbean English, Australian English, etc.

All of the many varieties of English have much in common. For example, the differences in grammar are usually small and the great majority of the vocabulary is shared by speakers of English everywhere. So where are the differences? As we pointed out in Unit 2, there are small differences in spelling. There are differences in vocabulary when words from another language are added or adapted for better communication. In idioms and in the choice of words there is a lot of variety, and the greatest difference of all is in accents.

Today, other Englishes are more and more accepted as people all over the world choose to speak, write, and do business inEnglish.

In this story from a Ghanaian writer, some expressions may seem unusual to those used to British and American English. Here are two examples, one of usage and the other of spelling:

1. …she would begin by just hinting one of her mothers on her mother's side…
2. Hei,…

With the guidance of your teacher, read through the text again and make a list of other examples and discuss in what way they vary from British or American English.

EXPLORING YOUR IDEAS

AN ACTIVITY FOR GROUP DISCUSSION, HOMEWORK, OR YOUR JOURNAL

Read these sentences and respond with your ideas and feelings. Discuss or write as much as possible because, as you do, more ideas will come to you.

1. …she said that things have changed.
2. I had been quite surprised and very relieved that you had such understanding.
3. …[education] takes away some very important part of understanding from them.
4. Then the boy and the girl looked at one another, burst out laughing…
5. …they do not prepare their own minds to handle such changes…

EXPLORING THE INTERNET

For information on Ghana and its many cultures, look at **www.ghana.com/republic**.

To find some information on the people of Ghana, recipes for the dishes mentioned in the story, and how to say a few words in Ga (a language of Ghana), go to **www.addo.ws**.

Learn how to make the Ghanaian dish, palaver sauce, through the "food" link at **www.ghana.co.uk**.

Read Ama Ata Aidoo's biography at **www.bbc.co.uk/worldservice/arts/features/womenwriters/ aidoo_life.shtml**. Click on "being a woman writer" for even more information on her work, writing style, and life events.

Learn about the history and traditions of African weddings at **www.africanweddingguide.com/history**.

We encourage you to do your own Internet search and share the sites you find with your classmates and with your teacher.

FOLLOW-UP ACTIVITIES

Choose one or more of the following activities to complete:

1. Imagine that you are one of the young people and write a letter or an email to a friend describing the fight between the mothers and the opinions of the grandmother.
2. Act out the discussion between the mothers about the wedding preparations.
3. Create a recipe book for special occasions, such as a wedding, by writing down a recipe and asking your classmates to add their own recipes.
4. Interview three persons who got married in their country and culture; then interview three persons who married outside their culture or country. Ask these questions:
   How did you meet your future husband/wife?
   Did you ask your family permission to marry or did you tell your family about your plans?
   Was there any opposition to your marriage?
   If so, how was it resolved?
   How was your wedding similar to and different from your parents' wedding?
   Add two questions of your own.
5. Illustrate the story with a drawing, a painting, a collage, or a photograph.
6. Give a presentation on Ama Ata Aidoo and her work in literature and politics.

If you enjoyed reading this story by Ama Ata Aidoo, we suggest that you read the other stories in her book, *The Girl Who Can and Other Stories.* See the acknowledgements page for publishing information.

Unit
9

CLOTHES
Chitra Banerjee Divakaruni

India
and the USA

"You are beautiful." His voice starts a flutter in my belly.

Unit 9

CLOTHES
Chitra Banerjee Divakaruni

India
and the USA

INTRODUCTION

Think about and/or discuss these questions:

1. How do you choose what to wear everyday?
2. What do your clothes say about you?
3. What kind of clothes would you or could you not wear?
4. As an adult, would you disobey your parents? Explain your answer.
5. What is a dream you have for the future?
6. What are three important qualities of a strong marriage?
7. What is the most important decision you have made in your life?

LIBRARY/INTERNET TASKS

Before you read the story:

1. Find information about the tradition of arranged marriages in India.
2. Find out which parts of the world Indians have immigrated to and why.
3. Look for information about the traditional clothes for men and women in India.

Clothes
Chitra Banerjee Divakaruni

Chitra Banerjee Divakaruni was born in India. She lived in Calcutta until she was sixteen, when she left to live in the United States. She has a Ph.D. from the University of California at Berkeley. This is an excerpt from "Clothes," a short story in her award-winning book, *Arranged Marriage.*

The bold words should be learned. The numbered words are explained to help you understand the story. Some words have more than one meaning. The meaning we give is the closest synonym.

Late at night I stand in front of our bedroom mirror trying on the clothes that Somesh has bought for me and smuggled in[1] past his parents. I model each one for him, walking back and forth[2], clasping[3] my hands behind my head, lips pouted[4], left hip thrust[5] out just like the models on TV while he **whispers** applause[6]. I'm breathless with suppressed[7] laughter (Father and Mother Sen must not hear us) and my cheeks are hot with the delicious excitement of conspiracy[8]. We've stuffed[9] a towel at the bottom of the door so no light will shine through.

whispers:
speaks in a low voice

1 smuggled in:
brought in secretly

2 back and forth:
up and down

3 clasping:
holding together

4 pouted: pushed out

5 thrust: pushed forward

6 applause:
admiration, approval

7 suppressed:
stopped, kept inside

8 conspiracy: secret plan

9 stuffed: pushed into

19 paperweight:
   heavy object for keeping
   papers in place

I'm wearing a pair of jeans now, marveling at[10] the curves of my hips and thighs, which have always been hidden under the flowing[11] lines of my saris[12]. I love the color, the same pale color as the *nayantara* flowers that grow in my parents' garden. The solid comforting weight. The jeans come with a close fitting T-shirt which outlines my breasts.

I **scold** Somesh to hide my embarrassed pleasure. He shouldn't have been so extravagant[13]. We can't afford it. He just smiles.

The T-shirt is sunrise-orange—the color, I decide, of joy, my new American life. Across the middle, in large black letters, is written *Great America*. I was sure the letters referred to[14] the country, but Somesh told me it is the name of an amusement park, a place where people go to have fun. I think it is a wonderful **concept**, novel[15]. Above the letters is a picture of a train. Only it's not a train, Somesh tells me, it's a roller coaster. He tries to explain how it moves, the **insane** speed, the **dizzy** ground falling away, he gives up. "I'll take you there, Mita sweetheart," he says, "as soon as we move to our own place."

That's our dream (mine more than his, I suspect[16])—moving out of this two-room apartment where it seems to me if we all breathed in at once, there would be no air left. Where I must cover my head with the edge of my Japan nylon sari (my expensive Indian ones are to be saved for special occasions—trips to the temple, Bengali New Year) and serve tea to the old women that come to visit Mother Sen, where like a good Indian wife I must never address my husband by his name. Where even in our bed we kiss **guiltily**, uneasily, listening for the giveaway creak[17] of springs. Sometimes I laugh to myself, thinking how **ironic** it is that after all my fears about America, my life has turned out to be no different from Deepali's or Radha's[18]. But at other times I feel caught in a world where everything is frozen in place, like a scene inside a glass paperweight[19]. It is a world so small that if I were to **stretch out** my arms, I would touch its cold unyielding[20] edges. I stand inside this glass world, watching helplessly as America **rushes** by, wanting to scream. Then **I'm ashamed**. Mita, I tell myself, you're growing westernized. Back home you'd never have felt this way.

We must be patient. I know that. Tactful[21], loving children. That is the Indian way. "I'm their life," Somesh tells me as we lie beside each other, lazy from lovemaking. He's not boasting[22], merely[23] stating a fact. "They've always been there when I've needed them. I could never abandon them at some old people's home." For a moment I feel **rage**. You're constantly thinking of them, I want to scream. But what about me? Then, I remember my own parents, Mother's hands cool on my sweat-drenched[24] body through nights of fever, Father teaching me to

guiltily:
with the feeling we have
done something bad

ironic: funny but strange

crisp: neat and clear

read, his fingers moving along the **crisp** black angles of the alphabet, transforming them magically into things I knew, water, dog, mango tree. I beat back[25] my unreasonable desire and nod agreement[26].

Somesh has bought me a cream blouse with a long brown skirt, like the inside and outside of an almond[27]. "For when you begin working," he says. But first he wants me to start college. Get a degree, perhaps in teaching. I picture myself in front of a classroom of girls with blond pigtails[28] and blue uniforms, like a scene from an English movie I saw long ago in Calcutta. They raise their hand respectfully when I ask a question. "Do you really think I can?" I ask. "Of course," he replies.

⁂ What does Somesh smuggle into the apartment?
⁂ What is Mita's dream?
⁂ How does she compare her life in the apartment with the world outside?
⁂ How does Somesh feel about his parents? How does Mita feel about them?
⁂ Why did Somesh buy Mita an American outfit?

I am gratified[29] he has such confidence in me. But I have another plan, a secret that I will divulge[30] to him once we move. What I really want is to work in the store. I want to stand behind the counter in the cream-and-brown set (color of earth, color of seeds) and ring up purchases. The register drawer will glide open. Confident, I will count out green dollars and silver quarters. Gleaming copper pennies. I will dust the jars of gilt-wrapped chocolates on the counter. Will **straighten**, on the far wall, posters of smiling young men raising their beer mugs to toast[31] scantily clad[32] redheads with huge spiky[33] eyelashes. (I have never visited the store—my in-laws don't consider it proper for a wife—but of course I know exactly what it looks like.) I will charm the customers with my smile, so they will return again and again just to hear me telling them to have a nice day.

Meanwhile, I **will** the store to make money for us. Quickly. Because when we move we'll be paying for two households. But so far it hasn't worked. They're running at a loss[34], Somesh tells me. They had to let the **hired help** go. This means most nights Somesh has to take the graveyard shift[35] (that horrible word, like a cold hand up my **spine**) because his partner refuses to.

"That bastard!" Somesh spat out[36] once. "Just because he put in more money he thinks he can order me around. I'll show him!" I was frightened by the vicious twist[37] of his mouth. Somehow I'd never imagined that he could be angry.

straighten: arrange neatly

will: secretly command

hired help: employees
spine:
line of bones in the back

25 beat back: push back

26 nod agreement:
   (move head to) say yes

27 almond:
   a flat nut with
   a sweet taste

28 pigtails:
   hair that is tied together
   at the sides of the head,
   tight braids

29 gratified: pleased

30 divulge: explain, reveal

31 toast: celebrate

32 scantily clad:
   almost naked

33 spiky: pointed

34 running at a loss:
   operating while
   losing money

35 graveyard shift:
   work period from
   midnight to morning

36 spat out: said in anger

37 vicious twist:
   angry movement

38 crouching:
    sitting on his heels

39 lacy:
    with a delicate decoration

40 outrageously: shockingly

41 flutter:
    little heartbeat movement

42 vain:
    too pleased with oneself

43 braids:
    three or more lengths
    of hair that are woven
    into one piece

44 escaped strands: free hair

45 camouflaged: hidden

46 sandalwood sachet:
    small bag of
    scented wood

47 purification bath:
    religious cleaning

48 voile:
    transparent material

49 bunch: come together

50 petticoat: half slip

51 clamp down: bite

52 fierce: violent

53 bangle: bracelet

Often Somesh leaves as soon as he has dinner and doesn't get back till after I have made morning tea for Father and Mother Sen. I lie mostly awake on those nights, picturing masked **intruders** crouching[38] in the shadowed back of the store, like I have seen on the police shows Father Sen sometimes watches. But Somesh insists that there's nothing to worry about, they have bars on the windows and a **burglar alarm**. "And remember," he says, "the extra cash will help us move out that much quicker."

I'm wearing a nightie now, my very first one. It's black and lacy[39], with a bit of a shine to it, and it **glides** over my hips to stop outrageously[40] at mid-thigh. My mouth is an O of surprise in the mirror, my legs long and pale and sleek from the hair remover I asked Somesh to buy me last week. The legs of a movie star. Somesh laughs at the look on my face, then says, "You're beautiful." His voice starts a flutter[41] in my belly.

"Do you really think so," I ask, mostly because I want to hear him say it again. No one has called me beautiful before. My father would have thought it **inappropriate**, my mother that it would make me vain[42].

Somesh draws me close. "Very beautiful," he whispers. "The most beautiful woman in the whole world." His eyes are not joking as they usually are. I want to turn off the light, but "Please," he says, "I want to keep seeing your face." His fingers are taking the pins from my hair, undoing my braids[43]. The escaped strands[44] fall on his face like dark rain. We have already decided where we will hide my new American clothes—the jeans and T-shirt camouflaged[45] on a hanger among Somesh's pants, the skirt set and the nightie at the bottom of my suitcase, a sandalwood sachet[46] tucked between them, waiting.

✳   ✳   ✳

I stand in the middle of our empty bedroom, my hair still wet from the purification bath[47], my back to the stripped bed I can't bear to look at. I hold in my hands a plain white sari I'm supposed to wear. I must hurry. Any minute now there'll be a knock at the door. They are afraid to leave me alone too long, afraid I might do something to myself.

The sari, a thick voile[48] that will bunch[49] around the waist when worn, is borrowed. White. **Widow's** color, color of endings. I try to tuck it in the top of the petticoat[50], but my fingers are **numb**, disobedient. It spills through them and there are waves and waves of white around my feet. I kick out in a sudden rage, but the sari is too soft, it gives too easily. I **grab** up an edge, clamp down[51] with my teeth and pull, feeling a fierce[52], bitter satisfaction when I hear it rip.

There is a cut, still stinging, on the side of my right arm, halfway to the elbow. It is from the bangle[53]-breaking ceremony. Old Mrs. Ghosh performed the ritual, since she is a widow, too. She took my hands in

intruders:
people who enter in secret

burglar alarm:
protection system
with a loud bell

glides:
runs smoothly, like water

inappropriate:
not right, improper

widow:
woman whose
husband is dead

numb: without feeling

grab: take suddenly

shattered:
broke into many pieces

hers and brought them down hard on the bedpost, so that the glass bangles I was wearing **shattered** and multicolored shards[54] flew out in every direction. Some landed on the body that was on the bed. I can't call it Somesh. He was gone already. She took an edge of the sheet and rubbed the red marriage mark off my forehead. She was crying. All the women in the room were crying except me. I watched them as though from the far end of a tunnel. Their flared[55] nostrils, the red-veined eyes, the runnels[56] of tears, salt-corrosive[57], down their cheeks.

* ✳ What is Mita's secret wish?
* ✳ Why does Somesh have to work the graveyard shift?
* ✳ What does Mita imagine?
* ✳ What can you say so far about the relationship between Mita and Somesh?
* ✳ What does Mita do to her white sari?
* ✳ What are the rituals for a new widow?

It happened last night. He was at the store. "It isn't too bad," he would tell me on the days when he was in a good mood. "Not too many customers. I can put my feet up and watch MTV[58] all night. I can sing along with Michael Jackson as loud as I want." He had a good voice, Somesh. Sometimes he would sing softly at night, lying in bed, holding me. Hindi songs of love, *Mere Sapnon Ki Tani*, queen of my dreams. (He would not sing American songs at home out of respect for his parents, who thought they were decadent[59].) I would feel his warm breath on my hair as I fell asleep.

Someone came into the store last night. He took all the money, even the little rolls of pennies I had helped Somesh make up. Before he left, he emptied the bullets from his gun into my husband's chest.

fists: closed hands

"Only thing is," Somesh would say about the night shifts, "I really miss you. I sit there and think of you asleep in bed. Do you know that when you sleep you make your hands into **fists**, like a baby? When we move out, will you come along some nights to keep me company?"

My in-laws are good people, kind. They made sure the body was covered before they let me into the room. When someone asked if my hair should be cut off, as they sometimes do with widows back home, they said no. They said I could stay at the apartment with Mrs. Ghosh if I didn't want to go to the crematorium[60]. They asked Dr. Das to give me

shivering:
trembling, shaking

something to calm me down when I couldn't stop **shivering**. They didn't say even once, as people would surely have in the village, that it was my bad luck brought death to their son so soon after his marriage.

54 multicolored shards: sharp pieces of many colors

55 flared: open

56 runnels: wet paths

57 salt-corrosive: biting with salt

58 MTV: a popular music channel on TV

59 decadent: immoral

60 crematorium: where dead bodies are burned

61 straggles:
walks in a disorderly way

62 sheer:
very thin and transparent

63 swept off: thrown off

64 silhouette:
outline, shadow

65 Dewar's: brand of whisky

66 yanked away:
pulled violently

67 crusting: dried on

68 *kurta* (Hindi):
male wedding clothes

69 musky aroma:
sweet, strong scent

70 sprinkled:
thrown gently, like water

71 tilting:
moving up to one side

72 seductive: attractive

73 drawing: pulling

They will probably go back to India now. There's nothing here for them anymore. They will want me to go with them. You're our daughter, they will say. Your home is with us, for as long as you want. *For the rest of your life.* The rest of my life. I can't think about that yet. It makes me dizzy. **Fragments** are flying through my head, multicolored and piercing sharp like bits of bangle glass.

I want you to go to college. Choose a career. I stand in front of a classroom of smiling children who love me in my cream-and-brown American dress. A faceless parade straggles[61] across my eyelids: all those customers at the store that I will never meet. The lace nightie, **fragrant** with sandalwood, waiting in its blackness inside my suitcase. The savings book where we have $3605.33. *Four thousand and we can move out, maybe next month.* The name of the panty hose I'd asked him to buy for my birthday: sheer[62] golden-beige. His lips, unexpectedly soft, woman-smooth. Elegant-necked wine bottles swept off[63] the shelves, shattering on the floor.

I know Somesh would not have tried to stop the gunman. I can picture his silhouette[64] against the lighted Dewar's[65] sign, hands raised. He is trying to find the right expression to put on his face, calm, reassuring, reasonable. *OK, take the money. No, I won't call the police.* His hands tremble just a little. His eyes darken **with disbelief** as his fingers touch his chest and come away wet.

I yanked away[66] the cover. I had to see. *Great America, a place where people go to have fun.* My breath roller-coasting through my body, my unlived life **gathering** itself into a scream. I'd expected blood, a lot of blood, the deep red-black of it crusting[67] his chest. But they must have cleaned him up at the hospital. He was dressed in his silk wedding *kurta*[68]. Against its warm **ivory** his face appeared remote, stern. The musky aroma[69] of his aftershave lotion that someone must have sprinkled[70] on his body. It didn't quite hide that other smell, thin, sour, metallic. The smell of death. The floor **shifted** under me, tilting[71] like a wave.

I'm lying on the floor now, on the spilled white sari, I feel sleepy, Or perhaps it is some other feeling that I don't have a word for. The sari is seductive[72]-soft, drawing[73] me into its folds.

fragments: pieces

fragrant: scented

with disbelief: not believing

gathering: coming together

ivory: cream color

shifted: moved

❋ What happens to Somesh?
❋ How is Mita treated by her in-laws? What do they expect her to do?
❋ How does Mita imagine Somesh's death?
❋ Describe Somesh's appearance after he is dead.

Sometimes, bathing at the lake, I would move away from my friends, their endless chatter. I'd swim toward the middle of the water with a lazy backstroke, gazing at the sky, its enormous blueness drawing me up until I felt weightless and dizzy. Once in a while there would be a plane, a small silver needle drawn through the clouds, in and out, until it disappeared. Sometimes the thought came to me, as I **floated** in the middle of the lake with the sun beating down on my closed eyelids, that it would be so easy to let go, to drop into the dim[74] brown world of mud, of water weeds[75] fine as hair.

Once I almost did it. I curled my body inward[76], tight as a fist, and felt it start to **sink**. The sun grew pale and shapeless; the water, suddenly cold, licked at the insides of my ears in welcome. But in the end, I couldn't.

They are knocking at the door now, calling my name. I pull myself off the floor, my body almost too heavy to lift up, as when one climbs out after a long swim. I'm surprised at how vividly[77] it comes to me, this memory I haven't called up in years: the desperate flailing[78] of arms and legs as I fought my way upward; the press of the water on me, heavy as **terror**; the wild animal **trapped** inside my chest, clawing[79] at my lungs. The day returning to me as searing[80] air, the way I drew it in, in, as though I would never have enough of it.

That's when I know I can't go back. I don't know yet how I'll manage, here in this new, dangerous land. I only know I must. Because all over India, at this very moment, widows in white saris are bowing their veiled heads, serving tea to their in-laws. Doves[81] with cut-off wings.

I am standing in front of the mirror now, gathering up the sari. I tuck in[82] the ripped end so it lies next to my skin, my secret. I make myself think of the store, although it hurts. Inside the refrigerated unit, blue milk cartons lined up by Somesh's hands. The exotic[83] smell of Hills Brothers coffee brewed black and strong, the glisten[84] of sugar-glazed **donuts** nestled[85] in tissue, the neon Budweiser emblem[86] winking[87] on and off like a **risky** invitation.

I straighten my shoulders and stand taller, take a deep breath. Air fills me—the same air that traveled through Somesh's lungs a little while ago. The thought is like an unexpected, intimate gift. I tilt my chin, readying myself for the **arguments** of the coming weeks, the remonstrations[88]. In the mirror a woman holds my gaze, her eyes apprehensive[89] yet **steady**. She wears a blouse and a skirt the color of almonds.

✳ Why does Mita remember her time at the lake?
✳ What decision does Mita make at the end of the story and why?

floated:
lay on the surface
of the water

sink: go down to the bottom

terror: great fear

trapped: caught

donuts: sweet pastries
risky: dangerous

arguments: discussions

steady: strong and balanced

74 dim: dark

75 weeds: plants

76 curled inward:
   rolled into a ball

77 vividly:
   clearly, realistically

78 flailing: wild movements

79 clawing: scratching

80 searing: burning

81 doves: birds of peace

82 tuck in: push in

83 exotic: strange, foreign

84 glisten: shine

85 nestled: held

86 Budweiser emblem:
   beer sign

87 winking: shining, flashing

88 remonstrations:
   objections, protests

89 apprehensive: worried

EXPLORING THE STORY

AN ACTIVITY FOR GROUP DISCUSSION, HOMEWORK, OR YOUR JOURNAL

A good writer will not only describe interesting characters and an interesting plot—what happens in the story—but will also provide extra ideas or opinions that are not always easy to see.

Read the questions below and think about them. Always go back to the story to find the answers to the questions.

1. There are several secrets in this story. What secrets do Somesh and Mita keep from his parents? What secret does Mita keep from Somesh? What is the final secret in the story?
2. When she thinks about her father and mother-in-law, Mita has "mixed feelings"; that is, what she should feel as a good daughter-in-law and her real feelings are not the same. Find some examples in the story.
3. In the story, Somesh and Mita never say, "I love you" or "I am happy." How do we know they have a happy marriage?
4. Why do you think Mita remembers almost drowning in India at the same time she prepares to wear her white widow's sari?
5. Why do you think the author chose to call this story "Clothes?" What is your opinion of the title?

EXPLORING THE VOCABULARY

Complete the following sentences with bold words from the story. Change the form of the word when necessary.

1. It's a new _____. I have never even heard of it before.
2. You should be _____ of yourself. How could you do such a thing?
3. Before the visitors arrive, I need to _____ the room.
4. When I hear ghost stories, I get a cold chill up my _____.
5. My grandfather died when he was quite young. Grandmother has been a _____ for many years.
6. Here, take my coat. You're _____.
7. I love to come home when my mother is baking a cake. The house smells so _____.

8. I remember having many _____ with my little
    sister when she took my things.
9. My mother used to _____ us when we made too
    much noise.
10. Who broke the window? The glass has _____
    into a thousand pieces.

*Now choose ten of the numbered words and write a sentence for
each one. You may copy sentences from your dictionary.*

EXPLORING THE LANGUAGE

LANGUAGE CHUNKS

Many students like to learn fixed expressions (words that usually go
together) and then use these "chunks" of language in speaking or writing.
This kind of learning is very common when you learn your first language.
We recommend that you learn these language chunks.

*Here is a list of chunks from "Clothes." Study them. They are
explained in the margins of the story.*

hired help	graveyard shift
burglar alarm	spat out
running at a loss	smuggled in
back and forth	nod agreement

*Now complete these sentences with one of the expressions, chang-
ing the form of the words when necessary.*

1. When the teacher asked me if I had been cheating, I was so
    ashamed I just _____.
2. My uncle was worried. He walked _____ all night
    trying to find a solution.
3. The teacher doesn't allow chewing gum. He told me to
    _____ it _____.
4. They had to close down the business because it was

    _____.
5. James had to work the _____ when he started
    his first job.

6. When James heard the _____, he called the police.
7. James was the _____. The police suspected him of the theft. He didn't do it.

EXPLORING THE WRITING

SEQUENCE OF EVENTS

A "sequence" of events is the order in which things are told in a story. Some authors follow a "chronological" order, that is, they tell the story in the order in which the events took place. In "Clothes," the author chooses to mix events of the past and the present, sometimes using the present tense even though she is writing about the recent past. Read the following sentences and number them in chronological order:

___ Somesh draws me close. "Very beautiful," he whispers.

___ I yanked away the cover.

___ Someone came into the store last night.

___ I curled my body inwards, tight as a fist, and felt it start to sink.

___ I am standing in front of the mirror now, gathering up the sari.

1. What effect do you think the author wants to achieve by not using a chronological sequence in the story?
2. Why do you think the author uses the present tense sometimes and other times the past tense when Mita speaks of the recent past? What does it tell you about her sense of reality?

EXPLORING YOUR IDEAS

AN ACTIVITY FOR GROUP DISCUSSION, HOMEWORK, OR YOUR JOURNAL

Read these sentences from the story and respond with your ideas and feelings. Discuss or write as much as possible because, as you do, more ideas will come to you.

1. I stand inside this glass world, watching helplessly as America rushes by, wanting to scream.
2. "Please," he says, "I want to keep seeing your face."
3. Before he left he emptied the bullets from his gun into my husband's chest.

4. Fragments are flying about my head, multicolored and piercing sharp like bits of bangle glass.

5. In the mirror a woman holds my gaze, her eyes apprehensive yet steady. She wears a blouse and skirt the color of almonds.

EXPLORING THE INTERNET

To find out many interesting facts about Hindu life, look at **www.hindunet.org** and **www.hinduwomen.org**.

You can look for news, maps, jobs, romance, and/or recipes related to India at **www.bengalonthenet.com**.

To see beautiful photographs of India, go to **www.culturefocus.com/india.htm**.

At **www.chitradivakaruni.com**, you'll find Chitra Banerjee Divakaruni's biography, as well as links to interviews with her and excerpts from her other books.

Learn about the different types of saris (sarees) worn by women in India at **www.massala.com/sari.htm**; then learn how to wear one at **www.maxwell.syr.edu/southasiacenter/saree/Sari.htm**.

Learn about the different types of marriage in India at **www.shaadi.com/shaadi_scene/indian_matrimony/index.php**.

We encourage you to do your own Internet search and share the sites you find with your classmates and your teacher.

FOLLOW-UP ACTIVITIES

Choose one or more of the following activities to complete:

1. Imagine you are Mita. Write a letter to your parents to explain why you decided to stay in the United States.
2. Look through the classified section of a newspaper and find three jobs that Mita could apply for.
3. Draw or paint a picture to illustrate the story.
4. Write a dialogue between Mita and Somesh's parents in which she tells them she will not return to India. Think about the arguments each side will make.
5. Write a summary of the story.
6. Write a page about Mita's life ten years after Somesh's death.

7. Write about an event that changed your life or about a difficult decision you had to make.
8. Give a presentation on one of these topics:
   a) Arranged marriages
   b) Learning to adapt to a new country
   c) The duties of children to their parents

If you enjoyed reading this story by Chitra Divakaruni, we suggest that you read the other stories in her book, *Arranged Marriage*. See the acknowledgements page for publishing information.

Unit

10

SECOND CLASS CITIZEN
Buchi Emecheta

Nigeria
and the United Kingdom

*This is your brainchild; you are the only one in this whole world
who could have produced this particular work, no one else could . . .*

Unit 10

SECOND CLASS CITIZEN
Buchi Emecheta

Nigeria
and the United Kingdom

INTRODUCTION

Think about and/or discuss these questions:

1. Are there differences in the ways men and women are educated in your country? If so, what are they?
2. Is it usual for women to work in your country? Are some jobs considered "men's work" and others "women's work?" If so, give some examples of each.
3. In general, how do husband and wife share the responsibilities of home and work in your culture? In your family? Who makes the important decisions?
4. In your culture, what is the position of women writers? What advantages and/or disadvantages do they have?
5. What does the expression "second-class citizen" mean? Who are the second-class citizens in your country?

LIBRARY/INTERNET TASKS

Before you read the story:

1. Find information about the history of Nigeria and its relationship with the United Kingdom. What is the role of English in Nigeria? Why?
2. Find out anything you can about Nigerian immigrants living in England. Are there any people from Nigeria or other parts of Africa living in your area? If so, why did they immigrate?

Second Class Citizen
Buchi Emecheta

This excerpt is from the autobiographical novel *Second Class Citizen*. The author, Buchi Emecheta, was born in Nigeria and moved to England in 1962. In the story, Adah, a young Nigerian woman, has written a book in English. She tries to avoid conflicts in her roles as a wife, a mother, and a writer, but finally must make a choice. The story takes place in London and actually happened to Buchi Emecheta. She has since left her husband.

The bold words should be learned. The numbered words are explained to help you understand the story. Some words have more than one meaning. The meaning we give is the closest synonym.

She was going to show *The Bride Price* to Francis, to show him that she could write and that she had not been wasting her time as he thought. But first she must take the manuscript[1] to her friends at the Chalk Farm Library.

Bill read it and so did Peggy and the others. She thought they would laugh and tell her it was a good first **attempt**. But Bill took it quite seriously. She should show it to somebody in publishing[2]! This scared Adah. She did not know anybody in publishing, she did not know whether she could type the whole lot. It was so enormous, that manuscript. The words, simple, not sophisticated[3] at all, kept pouring from her mind. She had written it, as if it were someone talking, talking fast, who would never stop. Now Bill said it was good, she should get it typed out. It was imperative[4] now that Adah should tell her Francis.

She renewed her books[5], tucked[6] them all neatly in between Bubu and Dada in the pram[7], mopped Vicky's running nose, and they all marched to Carlton School to collect Titi from the nursery[8]. But Adah was deep in thought as they crossed Haverstock Hill into Prince of Wales Road, pushing the pram with Vicky trotting[9] by her side, the sun shining in the sky, the day hot and merry like any day in Africa. People were passing her this way and that, all in colourful, sleeveless summer dresses, one or two old people sitting on the benches by the side of the Crescent in front of the pub smiling, showing their stiff dentures[10], their crooked hats[11] pulled down to shade their tired heads from the unusual sun. She walked into the Crescent where the smell of ripe tomatoes mingled[12] with the **odour** from the butcher's. But she saw none of this, her mind was turning over so fast. Could Peggy and Bill be right? Could she be a writer, a real one? Did she not feel totally **fulfilled** when she had completed the manuscript, just as if it was another baby she had had? 'I felt so fulfilled when I finished it, just as if I had just made another baby,' she had told Bill, and he had replied: 'But that is how writers feel. Their work is their brainchild. This is your **brainchild**; you are the only one in this whole world who could have produced that particular work, no one else could. If they tried it would just be an **imitation**. Books tell a great deal about the writers. It is like your own **particular** child.'

The phrase kept coming and going through Adah's mind. Brainchild, brainchild. Francis must see it. They might never publish it, she knew, but she was going to use that as a stepping stone[13]. She had always dreamed of becoming a writer, but she had told herself that writers knew so much that before she made her first attempt at collecting her knowledge into a book she would be at least forty. But now she had

attempt: try

odour (British spelling): odor, smell

fulfilled: contented, satisfied

brainchild: idea

imitation: bad copy
particular: special

done *The Bride Price*, as a joke at first, but realizing that she was serious as she scribbled[14] along. Now a few of her friends had read it and they said it was good.

- ▣ What do Adah's friends think of her book?
- ▣ What scares Adah? Why?
- ▣ How does Adah feel about her brainchild?
- ▣ Who does she want to show her book to?

She would study harder, then, to be a writer. But where would she start? There was such a lot, and such a diverse[15] lot, one had to know to be a writer. She could not write in any African language, so it must be English although English was not her mother tongue. Yes, it was the English language she was going to use. But she could not write those big, long, **twisting** words. Well, she might not be able to do those long, difficult words, but she was going to do her own **phrases** her own way. Adah's phrases, that's what they were going to be. But first she would need **guidance**. The simplest books she could think of were the Bible and the complete works of Shakespeare. Her Pa had taught her how to read by the Bible, St Matthew in the Bible, that part which said that there were fourteen **generations** after David before the birth of Christ. She **ended up** knowing most of the words of that part of the Bible **by heart**. As for Shakespeare, she had never stopped being fascinated[16] by him. It was going to be a lot of work but it could be done. Then she thought again. It was all right **mastering** the language; what of the **subject matter**? She could not just keep writing from memory, just like that, at random[17]. There must be a purpose, there must be a **pattern** somewhere. She could not find the answers to these questions at the time, but she knew they must be answered before she could write anything publishable. She was not just going to be a writer of ordinary novels. She would have too much competition in that line. She would have to specialize somehow, in some special thing. The only practical knowledge she had was **connected with** librarianship. You don't go about writing about how to file orders or shelve books according to Dewey[18] or the Library of Congress[19]! She could write about the people who came to borrow books, but she had to know about them. What **discipline** teaches people about people? **Psychology**? **Sociology**? **Anthropology** or history? She knew about the others, but what does a sociologist study? She would ask Francis. He ought to know. She would let him read the manuscript first, then she would ask, 'Where do you learn about people and what do they learn in sociology?'

twisting: difficult, complex

phrases: groups of words

guidance: help, advice

generations:
age groups;
i.e., grandparents,
parents, and children
are three generations

ended up: finished

by heart: from memory

mastering: learning

subject matter: main topic

pattern: organization

connected with: related to

discipline: subject of study

psychology:
study of the mind

sociology:
study of behavior of
people in groups

anthropology:
study of societies
and cultures

14 scribbled: wrote quickly

15 diverse: varied

16 fascinated:
very interested

17 at random:
without a plan

18 Dewey:
a system of
arranging books

19 Library of Congress:
a system of
arranging books

20 hired (British): rented

21 wailed: cried

22 barely tolerate: only just accept

23 breast-feed: feed a baby with milk from her breast

24 Flora Nwapa: a famous writer from Nigeria

25 for the time being: now

She told Francis about *The Bride Price* in the evening. But he replied that he would rather watch *The Saint* on the new television which they had hired[20]. Adah **pleaded**, and wailed[21] at him that it was good, that her friends at the library said so. He should please read it. She said that Bill thought it should be typed out, because it was good.

pleaded: asked, begged

Then Francis said, 'You keep forgetting that you are a woman and that you are black. The white man can barely tolerate[22] us men, to say nothing of brainless females like you who could think of nothing except how to breast-feed[23] her baby.'

'That may be so,' cried Adah, 'but people have read it. And they say it's good. Just read it, I want your **opinion**. Don't you know what it means to us if in the future I could be a writer?'

opinion: ideas

Francis laughed. Whatever was he going to hear next? A woman writer in his own house, in a white man's country?

'Well, Flora Nwapa[24] is black and she writes,' Adah **challenged**. 'I have seen her books in all the libraries where I worked.'

challenged: tested, dared

Francis did not reply to this. He was not going to read Adah's **rubbish** and that was that. Adah was hurt badly, but she said nothing. She simply took her books of 'rubbish' and placed them neatly where she kept the books she borrowed from the library that week. She would save up somehow and buy herself a typewriter, a second-hand one, one of those sold at the Crescent, and then she would type it all out. Meanwhile, she would keep them there and go on reading.

rubbish (British): trash

- Why does Adah decide to write in English?
- What is Adah's profession?
- Who is Francis and what does he think of Adah's writing?
- What does Adah plan to do?

The thought of all this **haunted** her like a bad dream. That Francis would not read her book was bad enough but that he had called it rubbish without doing so was a deeper hurt, and that he had said she would never be a writer because she was black and because she was a woman was like killing her **spirit**. She felt empty. What else was there for her to do now? It was plain to her that Francis could never tolerate an intelligent woman. She **blamed herself** again. They ought not to have come, then she would not have this **urge** to write now; her marriage would have been saved, at least for the time being[25], because she knew that some time later she was going to write. Librarianship was to her simply a stepping stone to bring her nearer to books which she dreamt she was going to write in the future, when she was forty.

haunted: troubled

spirit: life of the heart and mind

blamed herself: felt it was her mistake

urge: need

But in England, she had been made to start almost twenty years before her time. Her books might not be published until she was forty, but her first story had been completed. She could not go back now. She had known the feeling she had when she finished the story, she had tasted the fulfillment of seeing others read her work, and had felt an inner glow[26] that was indescribable[27] when other people said how much they had enjoyed reading it. Peggy had said, 'It was funny, I could not put it down. It was so **comical**.' Bill had said, 'You only, and nobody else, could have written that.' Well, there was no going back now. She must go forward.

The following Saturday she left the children with Francis and **dashed** to the Crescent to do her weekend shopping. They were all sleeping, Francis and the children and she did not **bother** to wake them up. The day was wet. The queues[28] at the Crescent were endless. Adah had to queue for meat, for ground rice, for semolina, and even okra had to be queued for. She had to stand, here and there, all over the place in the dripping rain. In the end, she was happy to rush home, all wet but with the **sense of relief** that her shopping had been done very early in the morning before the children were awake.

As she approached their landing[29], she could smell the odour of burning paper. She ran inside quickly, hoping and praying that Vicky had not set their room **on fire**. But inside, she saw that Vicky and the others were still asleep. It was Francis standing there by the stove, burning the paper. He saw her come in, her wet face **demanding** an **explanation**. But Francis went on burning the paper. They seldom talked to each other, the two of them. Not being able to bear the smell any longer, Adah had to speak.

She said, 'But, Francis, could you not have thrown all those papers you are burning into the **dustbin**, instead of creating this awful smell in the room?'

'I was afraid you'd dig them out of the bin. So I had to burn them,' was the **prompt** reply.

Adah became **curious**, **suspicious**, her heart beating faster.

'What are they, Francis? What are you burning? Letters? Who wrote them? Francis, what are you burning?'

Francis did not reply for a while, but went on feeding crumpled[30] sheets into the stove and watching the burnt papers flying lifelessly about the room like black birds. He blocked Adah's view on purpose with his broad back.

- Why is Adah hurt? Why does she blame herself?
- Approximately how old is Adah?
- Why is she determined to continue writing?
- What is Francis doing when Ada gets home from shopping?

comical: funny

dashed: ran, went fast
bother: trouble

sense of relief: feeling happy and satisfied

on fire: burning

demanding: asking for
explanation: details

dustbin (British): trash can

prompt: quick
curious: interested
suspicious: not trusting

26 inner glow: warm feeling inside
27 indescribable: impossible to describe
28 queues (British): lines of people waiting
29 landing: hallway, top of the stairs
30 crumpled: creased, wrinkled

31 posture: way of standing

32 triumphant:
    winning, victorious

33 annoyance:
    slight anger, irritation

34 agony: great pain

35 mournful: very sad

36 ceased: stopped

37 delight:
    give great pleasure to

38 garnished:
    added details to

39 gruesome:
    ugly and shocking

40 horsewhip:
    long thin piece of
    rope or leather used
    to hit animals

41 lash: beat

42 whipping: beating

43 smack his lips:
    make a noise of pleasure

44 glistening: shining

45 shudder: shake, shiver

46 heroic conquests:
    brave acts

47 smug: very satisfied

48 heroic deed: act of honor

Adah knew that posture[31] of Francis's, standing there, challenging her. When he turned his face round, she knew she had seen that triumphant[32] smile on his face before. Now she remembered. She had seen him smile like that when he was telling her how successful he had been in killing a monkey belonging to his friend. The friend had kept this monkey as a pet, to the annoyance[33] of everybody. Francis had bought rat poison, smeared it on a piece of bread and given it to the monkey. The monkey had died, but the agony[34] it went through, twisting **in pain**, the mournful[35] cry of the unfortunate animal, had never ceased[36] to delight[37] Francis. He had told this story to Adah so many times, garnished[38] with gruesome[39] **demonstrations** that Adah never forgot the way he smiled when telling it. There was another terrible story he had told Adah, smiling just like he was doing now. It was the story of a goat which his father had bought for Christmas. The goat was tied up in the backyard, and Francis had got the strongest horsewhip[40] he could find, and started to lash[41] this goat, telling it to tell him what two times two was. Adah had asked him whether it did not bother him, whipping[42] some animal that could neither talk nor know what two times two was. Francis would then smile and smack his little lips[43], his bright eyes glistening[44] behind his spectacles, and tell her that it did not matter at all; what mattered was that the goat would not answer his questions, so he had to be whipped for it. Adah remembered the whipping she got from her cousin Vincent, and she would remember how each stroke went burning into her skin, and would shudder[45] and tell Francis she did not want to listen to stories about his 'heroic conquests[46].'

Now Francis had that sickly smile on his face, and Adah guessed that he was smug[47] with some heroic deed[48]. He picked up the last sheet, and among the crumpled papers she saw the orange cover of one of the exercise books in which she had written her story. Then **reality** crashed into her mind. Francis was burning her story, he had burned it all. The story that she was **basing** her dream of becoming a writer **upon**. The story that she was going to show Titi and Vicky and Bubu and baby Dada when they grew up. She was going to tell them, she was going to say, 'Look, I wrote that when I was a young woman with my own hand and in the English language.' And she was sure that they were all going to laugh and their children were going to laugh too and say, 'Oh, Granny, you are so funny.'

Then she said to Francis, her voice small and tired, 'Bill called that story my brainchild. Do you hate so much, that you could kill my child? Because that is what you have done.'

in pain: suffering

demonstrations:
shows, displays

reality:
the world of experience,
not imagination

basing ... upon:
depending on

permitted: allowed

'I don't care if it is your child or not. I have read it, and my family would never be happy if a wife of mine was **permitted** to write a book like that.'

'And so you burnt it?'

'Can't you see that I have?'

That to Adah was the last straw[49]. Francis could kill her child. She could forgive him all he had done before, but not this.

49 last straw: end, limit

- Adah says that Francis had smiled the same way before. When?
- What are Francis's reasons for burning Adah's book?
- What is Adah's reaction?

EXPLORING THE STORY

AN ACTIVITY FOR GROUP DISCUSSION, HOMEWORK, OR YOUR JOURNAL

A good writer will not only describe interesting characters and an interesting plot—what happens in the story—but will also provide extra ideas or opinions that are not always easy to see.

Answer the activities and questions below. Always go back to the story to explain your answers.

1. There are parts in Adah's life that are in opposition to each other. Read the story again, and list the positive and negative parts of her life.

Positive	Negative
her children	her husband

Now look at each list carefully. In your opinion, which group has the most influence on Adah's life? Why?

2. There are many references to Adah's small children. What role do they play in her life?

3. How are Francis's and Adah's experiences with white people different? How do these differences affect their opinions about Adah's writing?

4. What gives Francis satisfaction? What power does he have over Adah? Who and what has power over him? What is your impression of him?
5. Adah blames herself for her bad marriage. What reasons does she give? Do you agree with her? Why or why not?
6. Who are the second-class citizens in this story and why?

EXPLORING THE VOCABULARY

Complete the following sentences with bold words from the story. Change the form of the word when necessary.

1. I _____ with my daughter not to drop out of school.
2. Children need the _____ of their parents in making decisions.
3. The _____ in my history class interested me the most.
4. As a female, my parents did not _____ me to study at a university.
5. When my children were very young, I made an _____ to study on my own, but I failed.
6. It was the _____ of most people at that time that mothers should be at home.
7. For _____ in our family, women stayed at home.
8. My father could _____ well-educated women. He did not know how to treat them.
9. I know it will be a _____, but I am going to study for a higher degree after my children grow up.
10. Do you think that my women friends have _____ get a good education?

Now choose ten of the numbered words and write a sentence for each one. You may copy sentences from your dictionary.

EXPLORING THE LANGUAGE

LANGUAGE CHUNKS

Many students like to learn fixed expressions (words that usually go together) and then use these "chunks" of language in speaking or writing. This kind of learning is very common when you learn your first language. We recommend that you learn these language chunks.

Here is a list of chunks from "Second Class Citizen." Study them. They are explained in the margins of the story.

by heart	stepping stone
ended up	at random
breast-feed	on fire
in pain	the last straw
smack his lips	inner glow
for the time being	sense of relief
heroic conquests	heroic deed

Now complete these sentences with one of the expressions, changing the form of the words when necessary.

1. Her first marriage was terrible; it was like she had chosen her husband _____.
2. Her husband divorced her and married five more times, each time leaving his wives _____.
3. He looked at each wife as a _____.
4. When he met a rich woman, he would _____ and decide to marry her.
5. After he cheated on her, wife number five said, "That's _____!"
6. Each wife was richer than the earlier ones. He used them as _____ to wealth.
7. _____, he is alone.
8. He has _____ very lonely and sad.

EXPLORING THE WRITING

COMPOUND WORDS

Many words in English are formed by putting two words together. An example in this story is: brain + child = brainchild. Sometimes, as in our example, the new word is written as one word; other times the two words are joined together by a hyphen (-), like this: "part-time."

The rules for writing one word or using a hyphen are complicated and have many exceptions, so using a dictionary is recommended. You will find that there are differences between British and American usages depending on which dictionary you use.

1. In this story, there are several compound words. Can you find them? Fill in the letters below.

   B __ __ __ __ __ - __ __ __ __ : how a baby eats

   H __ __ __ __ __ __ __ __ : used to hit an animal

   T __ __ __ __ __ __ __ __ __ : a machine that prints letters

   W __ __ __ __ __ __ : Saturday and Sunday

   B __ __ __ __ __ __ __ : area behind a house

   S __ __ __ __ __ - __ __ __ __ : used (not new)

   S __ __ __ __ __ - __ __ __ __ __ : less important

2. Use your dictionary to help you write compound words. Begin the compound words with the words given below.

   story _storybook, storyteller_ _____

   second _____

   week _____

   child _____

   book _____

   birth _____

   rain _____

EXPLORING YOUR IDEAS

AN ACTIVITY FOR GROUP DISCUSSION, HOMEWORK, OR YOUR JOURNAL

Read these sentences from the story and respond with your ideas and feelings. Discuss or write as much as possible because, as you do, more ideas will come to you.

1. This is your brainchild.
2. Adah's phrases, that's what they were going to be.
3. You keep forgetting you are a woman and that you are black.
4. Well, there was no going back now. She must go forward.
5. Do you hate me so much, that you could kill my child?

EXPLORING THE INTERNET

Find current information on Nigeria at **www.ngex.com**, where you can listen to music, send a card to a friend, and discover the latest news in sports.

For comprehensive information about Nigeria, go to **www.motherlandnigeria.com**, a site with details on the peoples of Nigeria, great links to Nigerian writer Flora Nwapa, and a good short biography of Buchi Emecheta (click on the "Notable Women" link).

Read more about Buchi Emecheta's life at **www.bbc.co.uk/worldservice/arts/features/womenwriters/emechetta_life.shtml**. You'll also find interviews with her and links to her work and writing style.

For information, news, and ideas shaping Black life in Modern Britain, see **www.chronicleworld.org**.

Discover the Women of Color Resource Center and listings of other organizations dedicated to improving the lives of women of color at **www.coloredgirls.org/pub/pub_directory_index_net.html**.

We encourage you to do your own Internet search and share the sites you find with your classmates and with your teacher.

FOLLOW-UP ACTIVITIES

Choose one or more of the following activities to complete:

1. Imagine that you are Adah. Write a letter to a close friend or family member explaining what happened. Ask for advice.
2. Imagine that you are the friend and respond to Adah's letter.
3. Interview a woman who is successful in her work.
   Ask her these questions:
   Why did you choose this profession?
   Did you meet any obstacles?
   Who helped you and how?
   Did anyone try to stop you?
   What success have you had?
   Add two questions of your own.
   Report the answers on an audiocassette or in a paper. You can also get together with other students and make a panel presentation comparing the answers you received.

4. Write and act out a dialogue between Bill (Adah's friend) and Francis (Adah's husband) in which each tries to convince the other that he is right about Adah's book.

5. Illustrate a passage (part of the story) from "Second Class Citizen." Explain your choice.

6. Write a letter to the *Views and Voices* authors telling them your response to Adah's story. The letter can be addressed to their publisher (see Alta's contact information at the beginning of the book).

7. Write a journal entry describing what kind of help and support you expect from the person you marry (or have married).

8. Do you have a brainchild or are you dreaming of one? Write an essay describing it.

9. In this story, moving to a new culture changes Adah's life.
   If you have moved to a new culture, write an essay on how it has changed your life. If you have not, interview someone who has and report on his or her experience.

10. Using the information you have in the story, imagine Adah's life five years later. What changes do you think will take place? Discuss or write a short essay.

If you enjoyed reading this excerpt from Buchi Emecheta's novel, we suggest that you read the whole book, *Second Class Citizen*. See the acknowledgements page for publishing information.

P
A
R
T

T
H
R
E
E

Culture Clash

My son is beginning to speak like the others here
in Louisiana… He doesn't speak Vietnamese at all
and my wife says not to worry about that. He's an American.

Robert Olen Butler, Crickets

Unit
11

THINGS FALL APART
Chinua Achebe

Nigeria

An 'evil forest' was, therefore, alive with sinister forces and powers of darkness.
It was such a forest that the rulers of Mbanta gave to the missionaries.

Unit 11

THINGS FALL APART
Chinua Achebe

Nigeria

INTRODUCTION

Think about and/or discuss these questions:

1. How many religions are there in your country? Name some of them.
2. Have you ever seen or met missionaries (people who want you to believe in their religion)? Describe your impressions of them.
3. In your religion, are there special ceremonies to honor your ancestors (members of your family who have died)? What are they?
4. In your community, are there places where strong religious powers may be found? If there are, can you describe them?
5. How important are religious beliefs to you? Does everyone in your family share the same beliefs?
6. What do you think about sons or daughters who change their religion from that of their parents?
7. Do you know anyone who has converted (changed religion)? Why did this person convert?

LIBRARY/INTERNET TASKS

Before you read the story:

1. Find information about the religions of people who lived in Nigeria before the European missionaries arrived.
2. Why and when did European missionaries first go to Africa?
3. What are the larger religious groups in Nigeria today?

Things Fall Apart
Chinua Achebe

Chinua Achebe is often called the father of modern African fiction. In addition to his famous novels, he has written many essays and several children's stories. This is chapter seventeen from his novel *Things Fall Apart*, which he had published at the age of 28. The story takes place long ago in Nigeria when white missionaries first came to Africa. It is a story of conflicts between groups, between people, and inside people.

The bold words should be learned. The numbered words are explained to help you understand the story. Some words have more than one meaning. The meaning we give is the closest synonym.

The **missionaries** spent their first four or five nights in the market-place, and went into the village in the morning to preach the gospel[1]. They asked who the king of the village was, but the villagers told them there was no king. 'We have men of high title[2] and the chief priests[3] and the elders[4],' they said.

It was not very easy getting the men of high title and the elders together after the excitement of the first day. But the missionaries persevered[5], and in the end they were received by the rulers of Mbanta. They asked for a **plot** of land to build their church.

Every clan[6] and village had its '**evil** forest'. In it were buried all those who died of the really evil diseases, like leprosy and smallpox. It was also the dumping ground[7] for the potent fetishes[8] of great medicine men when they died. An 'evil forest' was, therefore, alive with sinister forces[9] and powers of darkness. It was such a forest that the rulers of Mbanta gave to the missionaries. They did not really want them in their clan, and so they made them that offer which nobody in his right senses[10] would accept.

'They want a piece of land to build their shrine[11],' said Uchendu to his peers[12] when they **consulted** among themselves. He paused, and there was a murmur[13] of surprise and **disagreement**. 'Let us give them a portion[14] of the Evil Forest. They boast[15] about **victory** over death. Let us give them a real battlefield in which to show their victory.' They laughed and agreed, and sent for the missionaries, whom they had asked to leave them for a while so that they might 'whisper together'. They offered them as much of the Evil Forest as they cared to take. And to their greatest **amazement** the missionaries thanked them and burst into song[16].

'They do not understand.' said some of the elders. 'But they will understand when they go to their plot of land tomorrow morning.' And they dispersed[17].

The next morning the crazy men actually began to clear a part of the forest and to build their house. The inhabitants[18] of Mbanta expected them all to be dead within four days. The first day passed and the second and third and fourth, and none of them died. Everyone was **puzzled**. And then it became known that the white man's fetish had unbelievable **power**. It was said that he wore glasses on his eyes so that he could see and talk to evil spirits[19]. Not long after, he won his first three converts[20].

- Why do the missionaries want to meet the leaders?
- What kind of place do the leaders offer the missionaries and why?
- What is the explanation that local people give to show that nothing bad happened to the missionaries?
- How many people decide to convert to the new religion?

missionaries: people sent to teach religion

plot: piece of land
evil: bad, dangerous

consulted: discussed
disagreement: difference of opinion
victory: success

amazement: surprise

puzzled: confused, did not understand
power: strength

attracted to: interested in
dared not: was afraid to

headquarters: main offices

confident: sure

ancestors:
family members
who have died

approached: came nearer

pregnancies:
times when a woman
expects a child

critical: not pleased with

Although Nwoye had been **attracted to** the new faith[21] from the very first day, he kept it secret. He **dared not** go too near the missionaries for fear of his father. But whenever they came to preach in the open market-place or the village playground, Nwoye was there. And he was already beginning to know some of the simple stories they told.

'We have now built a church,' said Mr. Kiaga, the interpreter, who was now in charge of the infant congregation[22]. The white man had gone back to Umuofia, where he built his **headquarters** and from where he paid regular visits to Mr. Kiaga's congregation at Mbanta.

'We have now built a church,' said Mr. Kiaga 'and we want you all to come in every seventh day to worship[23] the true God.'

On the following Sunday, Nwoye passed and re-passed the little red-earth and thatch[24] building without summoning[25] enough courage to enter. He heard the voice of singing and although it came from a handful[26] of men it was loud and **confident**. Their church stood on a circular clearing[27] that looked like the open mouth of the Evil Forest. Was it waiting to snap its teeth together[28]? After passing and re-passing the church, Nwoye returned home.

It was well-known among the people of Mbanta that their gods and **ancestors** were sometimes long-suffering[29] and would deliberately[30] allow a man to go on defying[31] them. But even in such cases they set their limit at[32] seven market weeks or twenty-eight days. Beyond that limit no man was suffered[33] to go. And so excitement mounted[34] in the village as the seventh week **approached** since the impudent[35] missionaries built their church in the Evil Forest. The villagers were so certain about the doom[36] that awaited these men that one or two converts thought it wise to suspend their allegiance to[37] the new faith.

At last the day came by which all the missionaries should have died. But they were still alive, building a new red-earth and thatch house for their teacher, Mr. Kiaga. That week they won a handful more converts. And for the first time they had a woman. Her name was Mneka, the wife of Amadi, who was a prosperous[38] farmer. She was very heavy with child.

Nneka had had four previous **pregnancies** and childbirths. But each time she had borne twins[39], and they had been immediately thrown away. Her husband and his family were already becoming highly **critical** of such a woman and were not unduly perturbed[40] when they found that she had fled to join the Christians. It was a good riddance[41].

* Give two reasons why Nwoye does not immediately join the church.
* Why do some of the new members stop going to church?
* What happens when the missionaries do not die?
* Why does Nneka decide to join the church?

21 faith:
  strong belief,
  usually in religion

22 infant congregation:
  new church members

23 worship:
  show love and
  respect for a god

24 thatch: dried straw

25 summoning: finding

26 handful: few

27 circular clearing:
  round open area

28 snap its teeth together:
  bite

29 long-suffering:
  forgiving, patient

30 deliberately: on purpose

31 defying: refusing to obey

32 set their limit at:
  only allowed

33 suffered: allowed

34 mounted: grew

35 impudent: rude

36 doom: bad future

37 suspend their
  allegiance to:
  stop believing in

38 prosperous:
  rich and successful

39 twins:
  two children born
  at the same time to
  the same mother

40 unduly perturbed:
  very troubled, worried

41 a good riddance:
  good that she left

42 *obi*:
the large living quarters
of the head of the family

43 saluted: greeted

44 compound:
enclosed area with houses

45 overcome: filled

46 gripped: held hard

47 choking grip:
grip that stops someone
from breathing

48 dwarf: small

49 blessed: holy, sacred

50 forsakes: gives up, leaves

51 for my sake: for me

52 matchet: weapon

53 wipe out: kill

54 vile and miscreant gang:
evil and troublemaking
group

55 exile: being sent away

56 despicable:
low, without self-respect

One morning Okonkwo's cousin, Amikwu, was passing by the church on his way from the neighboring village, when he saw Nwoye among the Christians. He was greatly surprised, and when he got home he went straight to Okonkwo's hut and told him what he had seen. The women began to talk excitedly, but Okonkwo sat unmoved.

It was late afternoon before Nwoye returned. He went into the *obi* [42] and saluted [43] his father, but he did not answer. Nwoye turned around to walk into the inner compound [44] when his father, suddenly overcome [45] with **fury**, **sprang to his feet** and gripped [46] him by the neck.

'Where have you been?' he stammered.

Nwoye struggled to free himself from the choking grip [47].

'Answer me,' roared Okonkwo, 'before I kill you! He seized a heavy stick that lay on the dwarf [48] wall and hit him two or three **savage blows**.

'Answer me!' he roared again. Nwoye stood looking at him and did not say a word. The women were screaming outside, afraid to go in.

'Leave that boy at once!' said a voice in the outer compound. It was Okonwo's uncle Uchendu. 'Are you mad?'

Okonkwo did not answer. But he left hold of Nwoye, who walked away and never returned.

He went back to the church and told Mr. Kiaga that he had decided to go to Umuofia, where the white missionary had set up a school to teach young Christians to read and write.

Mr. Kiaga's joy was very great. 'Blessed [49] is he who forsakes [50] his father and his mother for my sake [51],' he intoned. 'Those that hear my words are my father and my mother.'

Nwoye did not fully understand. But he was happy to leave his father. He would return later to his mother and his brothers and sisters and convert them to the new faith.

* How does Okonkwo react to his cousin's news at first?
* What happens when Nwoye goes to visit his father?
* How does Mr. Kiaga respond to Nwoye's decision to leave his family?

As Okonkwo sat in his hut that night, gazing into a log fire, he **thought over the matter**. A sudden fury rose within him and he felt a strong **desire** to take up his matchet [52], go to the church and wipe out [53] the **entire** vile and miscreant gang [54]. But on further thought he told himself that Nnowye was not worth fighting for. Why, he cried in his heart, should he, Okonkwo, of all people, be **cursed** with such a son? He saw clearly in it the finger of his personal god or *chi*. For how else could he explain his great misfortune and exile [55] and now his despicable [56] son's behavior? Now that he had time to think of it, his son's

fury: great anger

sprang to his feet:
jumped to his feet

savage blows: violent hits

thought over the matter:
thought about it carefully

desire: wish

entire: whole
cursed: punished

abandon: give up, forget

prospect: expectation

ashes: dust left after a fire

resembled: looked like

crime stood out in its stark enormity[57]. To **abandon** the gods of one's father and go about with a lot of effeminate[58] men clucking like old hens[59] was the very depth of abomination[60]. Suppose when he died all his male children decided to follow Nwoye's steps and abandon their ancestors? Okonkwo felt a cold shudder[61] run through him at the terrible **prospect**, like the prospect of annihilation[62]. He saw himself and his father crowding round their ancestral shrine waiting in vain[63] for worship and sacrifice[64] and finding nothing but **ashes** of bygone days[65], and his children the while[66] praying to the white man's god. If such a thing were ever to happen, he, Okonkwo, would wipe them off the face of the earth.

Okonkwo was popularly called the 'Roaring Flame.' As he looked into the log fire he recalled the name. He was a flaming fire. How then could he have begotten[67] a son like Nwoye, degenerate[68] and effeminate? Perhaps he was not his son. No! he could not be. His wife has played him false[69]. He would teach her! But Nwoye **resembled** his grandfather, Unoka, who was Okonkwo's father. He pushed the thought out of his mind. He, Okonkwo, was called a flaming fire. How could he have begotten a woman for a son? At Nwoye's age Okonkwo had already become famous throughout Umuofia for his wrestling[70] and fearlessness[71].

He sighed heavily, and as if in sympathy[72] the smoldering log also sighed. And immediately Okonkwo's eyes were opened and he saw the whole matter clearly. Living fire begets[73] cold, impotent[74] ash. He sighed again, deeply.

- What does Okonkwo want to do to the Christians?
- What is the worst thing that his son does according to Okonkwo?
- How does Okonkwo finally explain his son's character?

EXPLORING THE STORY

AN ACTIVITY FOR GROUP DISCUSSION, HOMEWORK, OR YOUR JOURNAL

A good writer will not only have interesting characters and an interesting plot—what happens in the story—but will also give extra information or ideas that are not always easy to see.

Answer the following activities and questions. Always go back to the story to explain your answers.

1. At the beginning of the story, the conflict is between the missionaries and the local people because each group has different goals. What does each side want, and how do they think they will get what they want?

57 stark enormity:
extreme seriousness

58 effeminate:
acting like a woman,
being weak

59 clucking like old hens:
making noises
like a chicken

60 the very depth of
abomination:
horrible behavior

61 cold shudder: bad feeling

62 annihilation:
complete destruction

63 in vain: without any hope

64 sacrifice: something
offered to a god

65 bygone days: the past

66 the while:
at the same time

67 begotten (biblical):
given birth to

68 degenerate: immoral, bad

69 played him false:
been untrue

70 wrestling: fighting

71 fearlessness:
not being afraid

72 in sympathy:
agreeing with

73 begets: causes, makes

74 impotent: without power

2. The presence of the missionaries and their converts is a problem in Nwoye's family, but not in Mneka's family. Why does each family react differently? What does it tell you about the status (the importance) of men and women in that village? What other information do you have about men's and women's status in the village?

3. Nwoye is interested in the new religion, but he is also afraid to join. What does he like about the new religion? Why doesn't he convert immediately?

4. Okonkwo has many different strong emotions when he hears about Nwoye's conversion. Write the reason next to each of Okonkwo's emotions below. Use words from the text.

violence _____

disbelief _____

fear _____

pride _____

anger _____

revenge (hurting the person who has hurt you) _____

sadness _____

understanding _____

EXPLORING THE VOCABULARY

Complete the following sentences with bold words from the story. Change the form of the word when necessary.

1. In comic strips, the forces of _____ are usually beaten by the good guys.

2. The good guys in stories often have more _____ than the bad ones.

3. Some people are _____ to the bad guys more than the good ones.

4. During a fight, both sides deliver many _____.

5. Fights often start when there is _____ between two people.

6. One person will _____ another person with angry words and movements.

7. When people fight, both sides want _____.

8. People who are _____ and daring are often considered good fighters.

9. When Nick did not win the fight, he was _____.

10. We hope that, in the end, people will _____ their anger and make peace.

Now choose ten of the numbered words and write a sentence for each one. You may copy sentences from your dictionary.

EXPLORING THE LANGUAGE

LANGUAGE CHUNKS

Many students like to learn fixed expressions (words that usually go together) and then use these "chunks" of language in speaking or writing. This kind of learning is very common when you learn your first language. We recommend that you learn these language chunks.

Here is a list of chunks from "Things Fall Apart." Study them. They are explained in the margins of the story.

right senses	set limits
evil spirits	sprang to his feet
burst into song	clucking like hens
cold shudder	in vain
wipe out	good riddance
play him false	in sympathy
dumping ground	

Now complete these sentences with one of the expressions, changing the form of the words when necessary.

1. Some people are afraid to walk in a graveyard at night. They fear

   _____ .

2. When you send a card in English to someone who has lost a family member, you can write "_____ " before your signature.

3. She was happy when he left. In fact, she considered it a

   _____ .

4. I tried very hard to forget him; but my efforts were

   _____ .

5. If we are careless, we might _____ the things we need the most to survive.

6. The bay is polluted. It was a _____ for the waste from the factories.

7. They drank so much it took hours to get them back to their

   _____ .

8. In the old days in England, a gentleman _____ when a lady entered the room.

9. Parents must _____ to what their children can and cannot do.
10. When you mention war, a _____ goes down my spine.

EXPLORING THE WRITING

PREFIXES AND SUFFIXES

Prefixes and *suffixes* are groups of letters that are added at the beginning or at the end of a word and change the word's meaning. Here are a few examples:

The prefix *un-* means "not" as in *unmoved* and *unbelievable*.
The prefix *mis-* also means "not" as in *misunderstand* and *misfortune*.

Underline the correct meaning of these words, then check your answer with a dictionary.

1. unpleasant

   | weak | disagreeable | poor |

2. unpractical

   | fast | difficult | useless |

3. mistake

   | error | accident | share |

4. misplace

   | move | annoy | lose |

The suffix *-ness* indicates a noun as in *darkness*.
The suffix *-ment* also indicates a noun as in *excitement*.

Check your dictionary to see if you can form a new word by adding -ness or -ment to the following words:

law _____

mind _____

amaze _____

agree _____

move _____

weak _____

Sometimes, these letters are neither prefixes nor suffixes.

Use your dictionary and circle the words that are formed with a prefix or a suffix:

cement	mister
stillness	uncle
unclear	apartment
moment	harness
misjudge	

EXPLORING YOUR IDEAS

An Activity For Group Discussion, Homework, Or Your Journal

Read these sentences and respond with your ideas and feelings. Discuss or write as much as possible because, as you do, more ideas will come to you.

1. Let us give them a real battlefield in which to show their victory.
2. It was said that he wore glasses on his eyes so that he could see and talk to evil spirits.
3. Her husband and his family were already becoming highly critical of such a woman and were not unduly perturbed when they found that she had fled to join the Christians.
4. "Blessed is he that forsakes his father and his mother for my sake," he intoned.
5. Living fire begets cold, impotent ash.

EXPLORING THE INTERNET

These two sites will give you good general information on Nigeria and Chinua Achebe: **www.pbs.org/hopes/nigeria/index.html** and **www.scholars.nus.edu.sg/post/nigeria/nigeriaov.html**.

Would you like to send a postcard from Nigeria? You can do so at **www.nigeria.com** (click on "postcards" under the "messaging" link). You will also find news of all kinds concerning business, sports, and more.

Learn more about the Ibo ethnic group in Africa at **emuseum.mnsu.edu/cultural/oldworld/africa/iboculture.html**.

Deepen your understanding of African culture and view beautiful photographs of Africa at **www.mnh.si.edu/africanvoices**.

Read about and listen to a program on traditional religions in Africa at **www.bbc.co.uk/worldservice/africa/features/storyofafrica/index_ section6.shtml**.

We encourage you to do your own Internet search and share the sites you find with your classmates and with your teacher.

FOLLOW-UP ACTIVITIES

Choose one or more of the following activities to complete:

1. Imagine that you are Nwoye and write a letter to your father. Try to explain why you decided to become a Christian.
2. Draw or paint a picture of the Evil Forest and the church.
3. Give a talk or write an essay about Nigeria today.
4. Look at a photograph of Chinua Achebe. Write a description of his face and of his character as you imagine it based on his picture and writing.
5. In your journal, write your reactions to the chapter you read.
6. Write a dialogue between a parent and a child who wants to join a new religion.
7. Did you ever change your opinion on an important subject? Share your ideas with a partner or write about it.
8. Today, there are religious conflicts (serious disagreements) in many parts of the world. Where are some of these places? If you have experienced this type of conflict, how has it affected you? Write or speak about the issue.
9. A major problem for people in developing and postcolonial countries is how to hold onto their way of life. Many young people look to western cultures for their values and beliefs. Write an essay in which you take a stand either for tradition or change.
10. If you belong to a religion, who was responsible for your religious education and how did they teach you? If you are responsible for another person's religious education, explain what your responsibilities are and how you take care of them. Either write or speak about your experiences.

If you enjoyed reading this chapter from Chinua Achebe's novel, we suggest that you read the whole book, *Things Fall Apart.* See the acknowledgements page for publishing information.

Unit
12

LOOKING FOR A RAIN GOD
Bessie Head

Botswana

When he was very young and the customs of the ancestors
still ruled the land, he had been witness to a rain-making ceremony.

Unit 12

LOOKING FOR A RAIN GOD
Bessie Head

Botswana

INTRODUCTION

Think about and/or discuss these questions:

1. What do you know about Botswana?
2. What types of food are grown in your country?
3. Is the weather sometimes a problem for farmers in your country? Explain.
4. In your religion, what do people do when they have terrible problems?
5. In your country, what happens to someone who kills another person?

LIBRARY/INTERNET TASKS

Before you read the story:

1. Find maps of Botswana that show you:
   a) the climate
   b) the description of land—hills, valleys, bodies of water, etc.
   c) the agriculture
2. Read a short history of Botswana.
3. Learn something about the religions in Botswana today and in the past.

Looking for a Rain God

Bessie Head

One of Africa's best-known writers, Bessie Head was born in South Africa but spent most of her life in Botswana. Her mother was Scottish and her father was Black South African. She died at the age of 49 in 1986. The story *Looking for a Rain God* is from her book, *The Collector of Treasures*.

The bold words should be learned. The numbered words are explained to help you understand the story. Some words have more than one meaning. The meaning we give is the closest synonym.

plough:
prepare the land, turn over the soil

surface: top

It is lonely at the lands where the people go to **plough**. These lands are vast clearings[1] in the bush[2], and the wild bush is lonely too. Nearly all the lands are within walking distance from the village. In some parts of the bush where the underground water is very near to the **surface**, people made little rest camps for themselves and dug shallow wells[3] to quench[4] their thirst while on their journey to their own lands. They

1 vast clearings: large open spaces

2 bush: wild country

3 shallow wells: not very deep water holes

4 quench: stop

5 lush: rich green

6 tangled:
  twisted, not straight

7 springing up: growing

8 moss:
  small plant that
  grows on rocks

9 figs and berries: fruit

10 dismal: miserable, sad

11 thornbush country:
  very dry land

12 curled up:
  become curved, not flat

13 withered: dried

14 anguish: suffering, pain

15 cooking utensils:
  pots and pans

16 charlatans:
  people who sell
  false remedies

17 incanters:
  people paid to say magic
  words against bad luck

18 witch doctors:
  men and women
  who use magic

19 talismans:
  charms, magical objects

20 downpour: heavy rain

21 scanty: small, light

22 stirred: moved, awoke

23 hedged: surrounded

experienced all kinds of things once they left the village. They could rest at **shady** watering places full of lush[5], tangled[6] trees with **delicate** pale-gold and purple wildflowers springing up[7] between soft green moss[8] and the children could hunt around for wild figs and any berries[9] that might be **in season**. But from 1958, a seven-year **drought** fell upon the land and even the watering places began to look as dismal[10] as the dry open thornbush country[11]; the leaves of the trees curled up[12] and withered[13]; the moss became dry and hard and, under the tangled trees, the ground turned a powdery black and white, because there was no rain. People said rather **humorously** that if you tried to catch the rain in a cup it would fill only a teaspoon. Toward the beginning of the seventh year of drought, the summer had become an anguish[14] to live through. The air was so dry and **moisture**-free that it burned the skin. No one knew what to do to escape the heat and **tragedy** was in the air. At the beginning of that summer, a number of men just went out of their homes and hung themselves to death from trees. **The majority** of the people had lived off **crops**, but for two years past they had all returned from the lands with only their rolled-up blankets and cooking utensils[15]. Only the charlatans[16], incanters[17], and witch doctors[18] made a pile of money during that time because people were always turning to them **in desperation** for little talismans[19] and herbs to rub on the plough for the crops to grow and the rain to fall.

The rains were late that year. They came in early November with promise of good rain. It wasn't the full, steady downpour[20] of the years of good rain but thin, scanty[21], misty rain. It softened the earth and a rich growth of green things sprang up everywhere for the animals to eat. People were called to the center of the village to hear the **proclamation** of the beginning of the ploughing season; they stirred[22] themselves and whole families began to move off to the lands to plough.

* Describe the land before and after the drought.
* Why do the people go to witch doctors?
* Describe the rain that came after seven years of drought.

The family of the old man, Mokgobja, were among those who left early for the lands. They had a donkey **cart** and piled everything onto it, Mokgobja—who was over seventy years old; two girls, Neo and Boseyong; their mother Tiro and an unmarried sister, Nesta; and the father and **supporter** of the family, Ramadi, who drove the donkey cart. In the **rush** of the first hope of rain, the man, Ramadi, and the two women, cleared the lands of thornbush and then hedged[23] their vast

experienced:
went through, felt

shady: out of the sun

delicate:
weak, easily broken

in season: ready to eat

drought:
period of time without rain

humorously: jokingly

moisture:
wetness, water in the air

tragedy: disaster, failure

the majority: most

crops:
produce of grain
and grass for food

in desperation:
needing very badly

proclamation:
announcement, declaration

cart: vehicle with two wheels

supporter:
the one who earns
the money

rush: hurry, haste

protect:
look after, keep safe

insects: bugs with six legs

fled away: went away

bare: empty

dizzily: playfully

cruelty: unkindness

in despair:
in great pain and worry

producing: making

tones: sounds

exact imitation:
perfect copy

bottoms: buttocks, behinds

expressions:
looks on their faces

purchase: buy

strain: tension, stress

weird: strange

stamp their feet:
hit the ground
with their feet

lost their heads: gone mad

self-controlled:
in control of their feelings

maintain: keep

starvation:
hunger that brings death

ploughing area with this same thornbush to **protect** the future crop from the goats they had brought along for milk. They cleared out and deepened the old well with its pool of muddy water[24] and still in this light misty rain, Ramadi inspanned[25] two oxen and turned the earth over with a hand plough.

The land was ready and ploughed, waiting for the crops. At night, the earth was alive with **insects** singing and rustling about[26] in search of food. But suddenly, in mid-November, the rain flew away; the rain clouds **fled away** and left the sky **bare**. The sun danced **dizzily** in the sky, with a strange **cruelty**. Each day the land was covered in a haze of mist as the sun sucked up[27] the last drop of moisture out of the earth. The family sat down **in despair**, waiting and waiting. Their hopes had run so high; the goats had started **producing** milk, which they had eagerly[28] poured on their porridge[29], now they ate plain porridge with no milk. It was impossible to plant the corn, maize, pumpkin and watermelon seeds in the dry earth. They sat the whole day in the shadow of the huts and even stopped thinking, for the rain had fled away. Only the children, Neo and Boseyong, were quite happy in their little-girl world. They carried on with their games of making house like their mother and chattered[30] to each other in light, soft **tones**. They made children from sticks around which they tied rags[31], and scolded them severely[32] in an **exact imitation** of their own mother. Their voices could be heard scolding the day long: "You stupid thing, when I send you to draw water, why do you spill half out of the bucket!" "You stupid thing, Can't you mind[33] the porridge pot without letting the porridge burn!" And they would beat the rag dolls on their **bottoms** with severe **expressions**.

The adults paid no attention to this; they did not even hear the funny chatter; they sat waiting for rain; their nerves were stretched[34] to the breaking point willing the rain to fall out of the sky. Nothing was important, beyond[35] that. All their animals had been sold during the bad years to **purchase** food, and of all their herd[36] only two goats were left. It was the women in the family who finally broke down under the **strain** of waiting for rain. It was really the two women who caused the death of the little girls. Each night they started a **weird**, high-pitched wailing[37] that began on a low, mournful[38] note and whipped up to a frenzy[39]. Then they would **stamp their feet** and shout as though they had **lost their heads**. The men sat quiet and **self-controlled**; it was important for the men to **maintain** their self control at all times but their nerve was breaking too. They knew the women were haunted by[40] the **starvation** of the coming year.

24 muddy water:
   water mixed with dirt

25 inspanned:
   tied to the plough

26 rustling about:
   making noises

27 sucked up:
   took away, swallowed

28 eagerly: willingly, happily

29 porridge:
   soft food from cereal

30 chattered:
   talked, had conversations

31 rags: pieces of cloth

32 scolded them severely:
   spoke in angry voices

33 mind: take care of, watch

34 their nerves
   were stretched:
   they worried

35 beyond: except for

36 herd: a group of animals

37 high-pitched wailing:
   very loud crying

38 mournful: terribly sad

39 whipped up to a frenzy:
   was brought to madness

40 haunted by:
   worried and very
   scared because of

41 witness: observer

42 struggling to recall:
    trying hard to remember

43 consulting in whispers:
    discussing in low voices

44 sacrifice: killing

45 conviction: certainty

46 unshakable authority:
    complete control
    or power

47 smashed: destroyed

48 devouring: killing

49 overwhelmed:
    got control of

50 ashen: gray

51 occurred: happened

52 unease: discomfort

53 cloud of sorrow:
    deep sadness

54 assuaged:
    calmed down, relieved

55 ritual murder:
    religious killing

56 statute books:
    books of laws

57 stamped out: ended

❋ Who are the family members in the Mokgobja group?

❋ What do they do to prepare the land?

❋ What do the adults do when the rain stops?
    What do the little girls do?

❋ How do the two women behave? Why? What about the men?

Finally, an **ancient** memory stirred in the old man, Mokgobja. When he was very young and the **customs** of the **ancestors** still ruled the land, he had been witness[41] to a rain-making **ceremony**. And he came alive a little, struggling to recall[42] details which had been buried by years and years of **prayer** in a Christian church. As soon as the mists cleared a little, he began consulting in whispers[43] with his youngest son, Ramadi. There was, he said, a certain rain god who **accepted** only the sacrifice[44] of the bodies of children. Then the rain would fall; then the crops would grow, he said. He explained the **ritual** and as he talked, his memory became a conviction[45] and he began to talk with unshakable authority[46]. Ramadi's nerves were smashed[47] by the wailing of the women and soon the two men began whispering with the two women. The children continued their game: "You stupid thing, How could you have lost the money on the way to the shop! You must have been playing again!"

After it was all over and the bodies of the two little girls had been spread across the land, the rain did not fall. Instead, there was a deathly silence at night and the devouring[48] heat of the sun by day. A **terror**, **extreme** and deep, overwhelmed[49] the whole family. They packed, rolling their skin blankets and pots and fled back to the village.

People in the village soon noted the absence of the two little girls. They had died at the lands and were buried there, the family said. But people noticed their ashen[50], **terror-stricken** faces and a **murmur** arose. What had killed the children, they wanted to know? And the family replied they had just died. And people said among themselves that it was strange that the two deaths occurred[51] at the same time. And there was a feeling of great unease[52] at the unnatural look of the family. Soon the police came around. The family told them the same story of death and burial at the lands. They did not know what the children had died of. So the police asked to see the **graves**. At this the mother of the children broke down and told everything.

Throughout that terrible summer the story of the children hung like a dark cloud of sorrow[53] over the village, and the sorrow was not assuaged[54] when the old man and Ramadi were sentenced to death for ritual murder[55]. All they had on the statute books[56] was that ritual murder was against the law and must be stamped out[57] with the

ancient: very old

customs: traditions

ancestors:
family members
who have died

ceremony: religious event

prayer: talking to a god

accepted: received, allowed

ritual:
actions and words
during a ceremony

terror: terrible fear

extreme: very great

terror-stricken:
badly affected by fear

murmur: talk in low voices

graves:
places in the ground where
the dead are buried

death penalty:
legal killing of a criminal

inadmissible evidence:
facts not accepted
by a court of law

death penalty. The subtle[58] story of strain and starvation and break-down was **inadmissible evidence** at court; but all the people who lived off crops knew in their heart that only a hair's breadth[59] had saved them from sharing a fate[60] similar to that of the Mokgobja family. They could have killed something to make the rain fall.

58 subtle: complex, difficult

59 a hair's breadth:
the smallest chance

60 sharing a fate:
having the same problem

❀ What do the old man and his son talk about?
❀ What happens to the little girls? Why?
❀ What questions do the villagers and the police ask?
❀ What happens to the old man and his son?
❀ How do the other villagers feel about what happened?

EXPLORING THE STORY

AN ACTIVITY FOR GROUP DISCUSSION, HOMEWORK, OR YOUR JOURNAL

A good writer will not only describe interesting characters and an interesting plot—what happens in the story—but will also provide extra ideas or opinions that are not always easy to see.

Answer the activities and questions below. Always go back to the story to explain your answers.

1. One theme is control, that is, who or what has power over people. Look at the sentences and write the word that best expresses the ideas in the story.

   1. _____ control the life of the villagers.
      a) Children   b) The police   c) The sun and the rain

   2. _____ must have self control.
      a) The villagers   b) The children   c) The men

   3. The police use _____ to control the villagers.
      a) charlatans   b) the law   c) the old man

   4. _____ control the lives of the little girls.
      a) The authorities b) The villagers   c) The parents

   5. _____ controls the actions of the old man and his son.
      a) Fear   b) Love   c) Hope

   6. The villagers hoped they could control rain with the help of _____.
      a) incanters   b) hard work   c) the police

   In your opinion, who or what has the most control over the lives of the people in this story? Explain your answer.

2. Another theme is death. Death is everywhere in the story: the death of plants and animals; the men hanging themselves from trees; as well as the death of the little girls, the old man, and his son. From what you know in the story...

   a) Do you think the old man really remembers the ritual or not?

   b) Is the sacrifice of a child in this story more or less powerful than the sacrifice of an adult? Why or why not?

   c) The punishment of the old man and his son is according to the law. Do you think their punishment is just? Explain your answer.

3. The story says that what happened was the fault of the women. In this statement, do you think the author expresses her own opinion or the opinion of someone else. If so, who? Give reasons for your answer.

EXPLORING THE VOCABULARY

Complete the following sentences with bold words from the story. Change the form of the word when necessary.

1. _____ is a serious problem on many farms where there is not enough water.

2. Every country needs to _____ food to feed its people.

3. In some places in Africa, the climate is _____. It has very hot summers and very cold winters.

4. After a drought, many people die of _____.

5. In Africa, many people have great respect for their

   _____.

6. The _____ of worrying about the weather caused the farmers to be very unhappy.

7. Last year, there was too much rain in parts of Africa, and that led to _____ from floods to landslides.

8. Many farmers keep large dogs to _____ their animals.

9. Another problem for farmers is _____. They can destroy crops.

10. When their crops failed, they had to _____ food in the town.

Now choose ten of the numbered words and write a sentence for each one. You may copy sentences from your dictionary.

EXPLORING THE LANGUAGE

LANGUAGE CHUNKS

Many students like to learn fixed expressions (words that usually go together) and then use these "chunks" of language in speaking or writing. This kind of learning is very common when you learn your first language. We recommend that you learn these language chunks.

Here is a list of chunks from "Looking for a Rain God." Study them. They are explained in the margins of the story.

in season	springing up
curled up	in desperation
in despair	lost their heads
stamp their feet	rustling about
sucked up	fled away
high-pitched wailing	whipped up
haunted by	cloud of sorrow
a hair's breadth	sharing a fate

Now complete these sentences with one of the expressions, changing the form of the words when necessary.

1. When my little boy gets angry, he shouts and _____.

2. The animals _____ from the forest fire in fear.

3. I only buy fruit and vegetables _____. They taste better and cost less.

4. In the spring, it's so exciting to see new plants _____ in my garden.

5. Look at the dog. Her new puppies are _____ next to her for warmth and comfort.

6. After his mother died, he was _____ for months. No one could comfort him.

7. The storm's destruction left everyone under a _____.

8. He was _____ thoughts of losing all his money.

9. _____, I wrote my parents asking for money. They couldn't really afford it.

10. They were so desperate, I was afraid they might _____ and do something dangerous.

EXPLORING THE WRITING

Paragraphs

When you listen to a story, the voice of the narrator gives you many indications about what is happening in that story. In written language, the author must use other ways to communicate with you, the reader. For that reason, a short story or a chapter in a novel is usually divided into *paragraphs*. Authors use paragraphs to give you a signal you can see. A new paragraph tells you that the situation is about to change. It may introduce a new character or give you any other information that is necessary for your thorough understanding of what you are reading. As a reader, it is important for you to recognize this signal and pay attention to it.

In "Looking for a Rain God," the author has divided the text into nine paragraphs. In a few words, write down the information the author gives you in each paragraph.

Paragraph 1: <u>Description of the land; the drought; effect on the people</u>

Paragraph 2: <u>The rains that came that year</u>

Paragraph 3: <u>Introduction of the family</u>

Paragraph 4: <u>The rains stop; reactions of the adults and of the little girls</u>

Paragraph 5: _____

Paragraph 6: _____

Paragraph 7: _____

Paragraph 8: _____

Paragraph 9: _____

You will notice that the first paragraphs tell you what you need to know to understand what happens in the sixth paragraph—the sacrifice of the children. The following paragraphs explain the consequences of that action.

EXPLORING YOUR IDEAS

An Activity For Group Discussion, Homework, Or Your Journal

Read these sentences from the story and respond with your ideas and feelings. Discuss or write as much as possible because, as you do, more ideas will come to you.

1. Only the children, Neo and Boseyung, were quite happy in their little-girl world.
2. It was really the two women who caused the deaths of the little girls.
3. A terror, extreme and deep, overwhelmed the whole family.
4. …the story of the children hung like a dark cloud of sorrow over the village.
5. They could have killed to make the rain fall.

EXPLORING THE INTERNET

The Hunger Project is an organization committed to stopping world hunger. Visit the Africa section of its site and find out what you can do to help at **www.thp.org**.

To learn more about famine and drought in Africa, visit FEWS NET (Famine Early Warning System Network) at **www.fews.net/learning/youth**.

Keep updated on news in Africa through the leading Internet source, **www.allafrica.com**.

For information on traveling in Botswana, go to: **www.geographia.com/botswana** and **www.africaguide.com/country/botswana/photolib.htm** (photographs).

Do you know that Bessie Head called her house "Rain Clouds?" You will find a short biography of her and good links to other sites at: **www.ex.ac.uk/~ajsimoes/aflit/HeadEN.html**.

Botswana is the world's largest producer of diamonds. You can learn about the controversial issues surrounding diamond mining at **www.diamondsfordevelopment.com** and **www.nytimes.com/library/world/africa/040600africa-diamonds.html**.

We encourage you to do your own Internet search and share the sites you find with your classmates and with your teacher.

FOLLOW-UP ACTIVITIES

Choose one or more of the following activities to complete:

1. Find out everything you can about Botswana. Write about it and report your findings to the class.
2. Write a dialogue between two children as they play a game.
3. Tell about a time when you lived through a natural disaster like a flood, big storm, earthquake, or drought. How did you feel? How did other people feel? What did you learn? You can write your thoughts down or record them on tape.
4. Find out about Bessie Head in your library or on the Internet. Write the story of her life. Make sure you illustrate it with photographs of her.
5. Illustrate with a drawing, painting, or a collage what happened to the Mokgobja family.
6. Write a description of a landscape you know well.
7. Imagine you are a villager. Write a letter to the judge explaining why he should not order the death sentence. Suggest an alternative.
8. With some classmates, present reasons for and against the death penalty.
9. Write a short article for a daily newspaper reporting the events in "Looking for a Rain God."

If you enjoyed reading this story by Bessie Head, we suggest that you read the other stories in her book, *The Collector of Treasures*. See the acknowledgements page for publishing information.

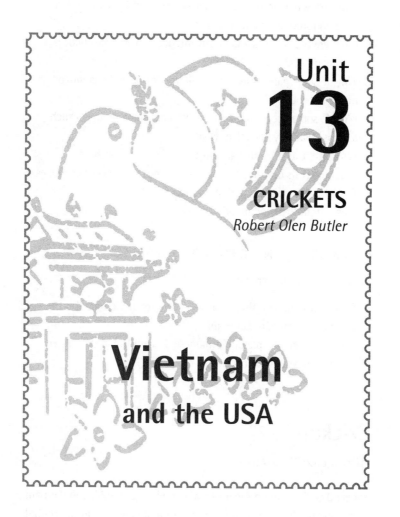

Unit
13

CRICKETS
Robert Olen Butler

Vietnam
and the USA

My son is beginning to speak like the others here in Louisiana…He doesn't speak Vietnamese at all and my wife says not to worry about that. He's an American.

Unit
13
CRICKETS
Robert Olen Butler

Vietnam
and the USA

INTRODUCTION

Think about and/or discuss these questions:

1. Talk to someone who has moved to a new country. What does he or she remember about the move?
2. Some teachers like to give new names to students who have immigrated. What do you think about this practice?
3. What are some reasons parents may find it difficult when their children forget their old country?
4. What are the benefits and disadvantages of being the child of immigrants?
5. Why do some parents like their children to speak the language of the old country?
6. Why do some people prefer to own brand-name products such as those made by Reebok or Nike?
7. What interests do you share with your father or mother?
8. What interests do you and your parents not share? Give examples.
9. Describe a game or song that your parents taught you. Was it from their childhood?

LIBRARY/INTERNET TASKS

Before you read the story:

1. Find information on the history and climate of Vietnam. Do the same for the state of Louisiana.
2. Find out where people of Vietnamese descent live in the United States or in your country.

Crickets
Robert Olen Butler

Robert Olen Butler is an American writer who was a soldier in Vietnam from 1969 to 1972. He is now a professor at a university in the United States. "Crickets" is a story taken from his book *A Good Scent from a Strange Mountain*, which won the Pulitzer Prize in 1993. This book is a collection of stories with Vietnamese characters. Crickets are small insects that jump and make noise with their legs.

1 decade: ten years

2 gold bullion: gold bars

3 tucked away: hidden away

4 bowler:
hard, round black hat

5 refinery:
oil treating factory

6 chemical engineer:
person who treats
petroleum

7 mustered into: taken into

8 unit dissolved:
army division disappeared

9 alleys:
narrow streets
between buildings

10 isolated: rare

11 pathetic: useless

12 gesture: movement

13 scorn: lack of respect

14 bayou: wetlands

15 rice paddies: fields of rice

16 delicate balance:
careful relationship

The bold words should be learned. The numbered words are explained to help you understand the story. Some words have more than one meaning. The meaning we give is the closest synonym.

They call me Ted where I work and they've called me that for over a decade[1] now and it still **bothers** me, although I'm not very happy about my real name being the same as the **former** President of the former Republic of Vietnam. Thieu is not an **uncommon** name in my homeland and my mother had nothing more in mind than a long-dead uncle when she gave it to me. But in Lake Charles, Louisiana, I am Ted. I guess the other Mr. Thieu has enough of my former country's former gold bullion[2] tucked away[3] so that in London, where he probably wears a bowler[4] and carries a rolled umbrella, nobody's calling him anything but Mr. Thieu.

I hear myself sometimes and I sound pretty **bitter**, I guess. But I don't let that out at the refinery[5], where I'm the best chemical engineer[6] they've got and they even **admit** it once in a while. They're good-hearted people, really. I've done enough fighting in my life. I was eighteen when Saigon fell and I was only recently mustered into[7] the Army, and when my unit dissolved[8] and everybody ran, I **stripped off** my uniform and put on my **civilian clothes** again and I threw rocks at the North's tanks when they rolled through the streets. Very few of my people did **likewise**. I stayed in the mouths of alleys[9] so I could run and then return and throw more rocks, but because what I did seemed so isolated[10] and so pathetic[11] a gesture[12], the gunners in the tanks didn't even take notice. But I didn't care about their scorn[13]. At least my right arm had said no to them.

And then there were Thai **pirates** in the South China Sea and idiots running the **refugee centers** and more idiots running the agencies in the U.S. to find a place for me and my new **bride** who braved with me the midnight escape by boat and the terrible sea and all the rest. We ended up here in the flat bayou[14] land of Louisiana, where there are rice paddies[15] and where the water and the land are in the most delicate balance[16] with each other, very much like the Mekong Delta, where I grew up. These people who work around me are good people and maybe they call me Ted because they want to think of me as one of them, though sometimes it bothers me that these men are so much bigger than me. I am the size of a woman in this country and these American men are all **massive** and they speak so slowly, even to one another, even though English is their native language. I've heard New Yorkers on television and I speak as fast as they do.

bothers: troubles, irritates

former: earlier

uncommon: rare, unusual

bitter: angry

admit: say

stripped off: took off

civilian clothes: everyday clothes

likewise: the same

pirates: thieves at sea

refugee centers: places where people who are forced to leave their homes stay

bride: recently married woman

massive: big and heavy

My son is beginning to speak like the others here in Louisiana. He is ten, the product of the first night my wife and I spent in Lake Charles, in a cheap motel with sky outside red from the refineries. He is proud to have been born in America, and when he leaves us in the morning to walk to Catholic school, he says, "Have a good day, y'all[17]." Sometimes I say goodbye to him in Vietnamese and he wrinkles his nose[18] at me and says, "Aw, Pop," like I'd just cracked a corny joke[19]. He doesn't speak Vietnamese at all and my wife says not to worry about that. He's an American.

♭ Why does the narrator have two names?
♭ What happened to Ted when he was eighteen?
♭ How did Ted and his wife leave Vietnam?
♭ Where do they live now and what does Ted do?
♭ How does Ted feel about the Americans in Louisiana?

But I do worry about that, though I understand why I should be content. I even understood ten years ago, so much so that I agreed with my wife and gave my son an American name. Bill. Bill and his father Ted. But this past summer I found my son **hanging around** the house bored in the middle of vacation and I was suddenly his father Thieu with a wonderful idea for him. It was an idea that had come to me in the first week of every February we'd been in Lake Charles, because that's when the **crickets** always begin to crow[20] here. This place is rich in crickets, which always makes me think of my own childhood in Vietnam. But I never said anything to my son until last summer.

I came to him after watching him slouch[21] around the yard one Sunday pulling the Spanish moss[22] off the lowest branches of our big oak tree and then throwing rocks against the stop sign on our corner. "Do you want to do something fun?" I said to him.

"Sure, Pop," he said, though there was a certain **suspicion** in his voice, like he didn't trust me on the subject of fun. He threw all the rocks at once that were left in his hand and the stop sign shivered[23] at their **impact**.

I said, "If you keep that up, they will arrest me for the **destruction** of city property and then they will deport us all[24]."

My son laughed at this. I, of course, knew that he would know I was bluffing[25]. I didn't want to be too hard on him for the boyish impulses[26] that I myself had found to be so **satisfying** when I was young, especially since I was about to share something of my own childhood with him.

"So what've you got, Pop?" my son asked me.

"Fighting crickets," I said.

"What?"

hanging around:
not doing anything

crickets:
small insects that jump and make singing noises with their legs

suspicion: lack of trust

impact: force
destruction: damage

satisfying: pleasing

17 y'all (Southern United States):
you all

18 wrinkles his nose:
an expression to show dislike

19 cracked a corny joke:
told an old joke

20 crow: sing

21 slouch: not do much

22 moss:
plant that grows on trees and rocks

23 shivered: moved

24 deport us all:
make us all leave the country

25 bluffing: not serious

26 impulses:
desires, instincts

27 devoted: faithful, loyal

28 mighty clash: great fight

29 cartoons:
    animated TV programs
    for children

30 frame of mind: mood

31 ploy: trick

32 cocked: turned

33 porch:
    area with a floor and
    roof attached to the
    outside of a house

34 prowl the undergrowth:
    search the bushes

35 agitation: worry

36 flicking: tapping

37 antennas:
    feelers on an insect's head

38 sliver: thin piece

39 stable: group

40 squirming:
    twisting and turning

41 had run its course:
    no longer interested him

42 urge to challenge:
    wanting to question

43 absorb: interest

44 cut to the chase:
    got to the point

45 gravity: seriousness

46 James Earl Jones:
    an actor with a
    deep voice

47 scrabble of panic:
    sudden feeling of fear

48 despair: give up

49 charcoal: dark gray

50 tunnel: channel or tube

51 cowling: shell

52 twirl: turn

Now, my son was like any of his fellow ten-year-olds, devoted[27] to superheroes and the mighty clash[28] of good and **evil** in all of its **high-tech** forms in the Saturday-morning cartoons[29]. Just to make sure he was in the right frame of mind[30], I explained it to him with one word, "Cricketmen," and I thought this was a pretty good ploy[31]. He cocked[32] his head in interest and I took him to the side porch[33] and sat him down and I explained.

I told him how, when I was a boy, my friends and I would prowl the undergrowth[34] and **capture** crickets and keep them in matchboxes. We would feed them leaves and bits of watermelon and bean sprouts, and we'd train them to fight by keeping them in a constant state of agitation[35] by blowing on them and gently flicking[36] the end of their antennas[37] with a sliver[38] of wood. So each of us would have a stable[39] of fighting crickets, and there were two kinds.

At this point my son was squirming[40] a little bit and his eyes were shifting away into the yard and I knew my Cricketmen trick had run its course[41]. I fought back the urge to challenge[42] his set of interests. Why should the stiff and foolish fights of his cartoon characters absorb[43] him and the real clash—real life and death—that went on in the natural world bore him? But I realized that I hadn't cut to the chase[44] yet, as they say on TV. "They fight to the death," I said with as much gravity[45] as I could put into my voice, like I was James Earl Jones[46].

The **announcement** won me a **glance** and a brief lift of his eyebrows. This gave me a little scrabble of panic[47], because I still hadn't told him about the two types of crickets and I suddenly knew that was a real important part for me. I tried not to despair[48] at his understanding and I put my hands on his shoulders and turned him around to face me. "Listen," I said "You need to understand this if you are to have fighting crickets. There are two types, and all of us had some of each. One type we called the charcoal[49] crickets. These were very large and strong, but they were slow and could become **confused**. The other type was small and brown and we called them fire crickets. They weren't as strong, but they were very smart and quick."

"So who would win?" my son said.

"Sometimes one and sometimes the other. The fights were very long and full of **hard struggle**. We'd have a little tunnel[50] made of paper and we'd slip a sliver of wood under the cowling[51] of our cricket's head to make him mad and we'd twirl[52] him by his antenna, and then we'd each put our cricket into the tunnel at opposite ends. Inside, they'd approach each other and begin to fight and then we'd lift the paper tunnel and watch."

evil: bad

high-tech: modern

capture: catch

announcement: statement

glance: quick look

confused: unclear

hard struggle: fighting

- What do you know about Ted's son?
- What does Bill like to do on Saturday mornings?
- What game did Ted play when he was a boy in Vietnam?
- Why does he try to teach his son the same game?

neat (slang): great

enthusiasm: excitement

at best:
at the most, no more than

crawled:
moved slowly on
hands knees

grab: catch and hold tight

hose faucet:
something you turn off
and on to control the flow
of water from a rubber or
plastic tube

bush: large plant

disappointment: lost hope

force: strength

sneakers: sports shoes

ruined: damaged, destroyed

slammed: banged

"Sounds **neat**," my son said, though his **enthusiasm** was, **at best**, moderate[53], and I knew I had to act quickly.

So we got a shoe box and we started looking for crickets. It's better at night, but I knew for sure his interest wouldn't last that long. Our house is up on blocks because of the high water table[54] in town and we **crawled** along the edge, pulling back the bigger tufts[55] of grass and turning over rocks. It was one of the rocks that gave us our first crickets, and my son saw them and cried in my ear, "There, there," but he waited for me to **grab** them. I cupped[56] first one then the other and dropped them into the shoe box and felt a vague[57] disappointment, not so much because it was clear that my boy did not want to touch the insects, but that they were both the big black ones, the charcoal crickets. We crawled on and we found another one in the grass and another sitting in the muddy[58] shadow of the house behind the **hose faucet** and then we caught two more under an azalea **bush**.

"Isn't that enough?" my son demanded. "How many do we need?"

I sat with my back against the house and put the shoe box in my lap and my boy sat beside me, his head stretching this way so he could look into the box. There was no more vagueness to my feeling. I was actually weak with **disappointment** because all six of these were charcoal crickets, big and inert[59] and just looking around like they didn't even know anything was wrong.

"Oh, no," my son said with real **force**, and for a second I thought he had read my mind and shared my feeling, but I looked at him and he was pointing at the toes of his white **sneakers**. "My Reeboks are **ruined**!" he cried, and on the toe of each sneaker was a smudge[60] of grass.

I glanced back into the box and the crickets had not moved and I looked at my son and he was staring at his sneakers. "Listen," I said, "this was a big mistake. You can go and do something else."

He jumped up at once. "Do you think Mom can clean these?" he said. "Sure," I said, "Sure."

He was gone at once and the side door **slammed** and I put the box on the grass. But I didn't go in. I got back on my hands and knees and circled the entire house and then I turned over every stone in the yard and dug around all the trees. I found probably two dozen more crickets, but they were all the same. In Louisiana there are rice paddies and

53 moderate: average

54 water table: water level

55 tufts: bunches, groups

56 cupped:
    caught with hands
    like a cup

57 vague: unclear

58 muddy: wet dirt

59 inert: still, unmoving

60 smudge: stain, smear

some of the bayous look like the Delta, but many of the birds are different, and why shouldn't the insects be different, too? This is another country, after all. It was just funny about the fire crickets. All of us kids **rooted for** them, even if we were fighting with one of our own charcoal crickets. A fire cricket was a very **precious** and admirable[61] thing.

rooted for: encouraged

precious: valuable

The next morning my son stood before me as I finished my breakfast and once he had my attention, he looked down at his feet, drawing my eyes down as well, "See? " he said. "Mom got them clean."

Then he was out the door and I called after him, "See you later, Bill."

- ❧ How do they catch the crickets?
- ❧ What is Bill's attitude towards the game?
- ❧ How does Bill react to his father's plan?
- ❧ What happens that upsets the boy?

EXPLORING THE STORY

AN ACTIVITY FOR GROUP DISCUSSION, HOMEWORK, OR YOUR JOURNAL

A good writer will not only describe interesting characters and an interesting plot—what happens in the story—but will also provide extra ideas or opinions that are not always easy to see.

Read the questions below and think about them. Always go back to the story to explain your answers.

1. Both father and son throw rocks in this story. Think about the time, place, and reasons for their rock throwing. Can you explain the differences?
2. How does Ted compare himself to the American men with whom he works? Think about the descriptions of the two types of crickets in the story. Can you see a connection between the fighting crickets and the men fighting in the Vietnam war? What type of cricket is Ted? And Bill? Explain your answers.
3. From the information we have in the story, what can you tell about Ted's wife? In what way are Ted and his wife different? Do you think Ted is a good father? Is he a happy father?
4. The author tells the story as if he were Ted, using "I" and giving much information about Ted's thoughts and feelings. Can you imagine what Bill thinks and feels while his father tells him about the crickets? Give examples.
5. Is "Crickets" a good title? Why not "Cricket" or "Ted and Bill?" Can you think of other possible titles?

EXPLORING THE VOCABULARY

Complete the following sentences with bold words from the story.
Change the form of the word when necessary

1. Lee failed the test, and it was a _____
   disappointment for him and his family.
2. It was so quiet. Then I heard the _____ of a
   car door.
3. The police did not _____ the thief. She is still free.
4. The dog _____ the ball and ran away with it.
5. They asked her so many questions that they
   _____ her. She could not answer.
6. When Jorge came in, he _____ around the room.
   He saw the stolen tennis racket on the bed.
7. The thief _____ that he had stolen the tennis
   racket.
8. After _____ of abuse, the government is finally
   learning to listen to its people.
9. _____ make a noise by rubbing their front wings
   together.
10. Heavy rain _____ the crops.

Now choose ten of the numbered words and write a sentence for
each one. You may copy sentences from your dictionary.

EXPLORING THE LANGUAGE

LANGUAGE CHUNKS

Many students like to learn fixed expressions (words that usually go
together) and then use these "chunks" of language in speaking or writing.
This kind of learning is very common when you learn your first language.
We recommend that you learn these language chunks.

Here is a list of some of chunks from the story "Crickets." Study
them. They are explained in the margins.

civilian clothes	stripped off
chemical engineer	refugee centers
rice paddies	cracked a corny joke
hanging around	hard struggle
at best	rooted for

Now complete these sentences with one of the expressions, changing the form of the words when necessary.

1. When our family first arrived in the United States, we were sent to a _____.
2. After three years in the army, Fatima was glad to wear _____ again.
3. Why are you _____? Don't you have homework to do?
4. The Walker family had a _____ to make a living when they moved to London.
5. Many people who visit Asian countries talk about the brilliant green of the _____.
6. In Russia, Olga studied to be a _____, but found it hard to find a job in the West.
7. When we go to a basketball game, we always _____ our home team.
8. My teenage children have no patience when I _____. They don't even smile.
9. I'm sorry I can't lend you $5,000; _____, I can let you have $500.
10. Maria saw the child fall in. She _____ her clothes and jumped into the water to save him.

EXPLORING THE WRITING

IMAGERY

How language is used makes the difference between good and great writing. One way the author can communicate with the reader is to choose words that create images in the reader's mind. The sentence below illustrates this idea.

I stayed in *the mouths of* alleys so I could run and then return with more rocks…

If you take out the italicized words, there is no change in the message of the story. The writer adds "the mouths of" to create a picture in the mind of the reader. When Ted runs out in the light, the mouth is open; when he runs back to hide in the shadows of the alley, it seems like a closed mouth that hides and protects him. This image adds drama to the story—it helps you feel the danger of the situation.

Now compare the following pair of sentences. The one with italics is from the story. Write down or discuss how the author's choice of words helps the reader share Ted's feelings.

This gave me a *little scrabble* of panic.
This made me feel very nervous.

Find two more examples of imagery in this story. Share them with your classmates and discuss how they help make the story more interesting.

EXPLORING YOUR IDEAS

AN ACTIVITY FOR GROUP DISCUSSION, HOMEWORK, OR YOUR JOURNAL

Read these sentences from the story and respond with your ideas and feelings. Discuss or write as much as possible because, as you do, more ideas will come to you.

1. "They call me Ted where I work and they've called me that for over a decade now and it still bothers me..."
2. He doesn't speak Vietnamese at all and my wife says not to worry about that. He's an American.
3. "Oh, no," my son said with real force, and for a second I thought he had read my mind and shared my feeling, but I looked at him and he was pointing at the toes of his white sneakers.
4. A fire cricket was a very precious and admirable thing.

EXPLORING THE INTERNET

What makes a good fighting cricket? See photographs of fighting crickets and read an interesting article on the cricket fighting season in China at **pub18.ezboard.com/fbalkansfrm9.showMessage?topicID=3.topic**.

The Vietnamese Boat People Connection at **www.boatpeople.com** has a lot of information about the dangerous exodus of hundreds of thousands of Vietnamese refugees, as well as several stories written by Vietnamese immigrants.

At **www.vietscape.com/travel/mekong** you can view pictures of the Mekong River Delta.

Do you know that sometimes Robert Olen Butler rewrites a sentence 10 to 12 times to get it right? Read an interview with Robert Olen Butler at **www.etext.org/Zines/Critique/writing/butler.html**.

Do you know what your name means? **www.eponym.org** has information about names from all over the world. Can you find yours?

We encourage you to do your own Internet search and share the sites you find with your classmates and with your teacher.

FOLLOW-UP ACTIVITIES

Choose one or more of the following activities to complete:

1. Write an essay or talk about what happened either from Bill's or from Ted's wife's point of view.
2. Explain why so many Vietnamese people left their country to settle in other parts of the world. Make a panel presentation to your class or write an essay on the topic.
3. Compare and contrast the Mekong Delta in Vietnam with the flat bayou land of Louisiana in the United States.
4. Illustrate the story with a drawing, painting, or a photograph. Explain your choice of scene.
5. Interview someone who has moved to a new country or city.
   Ask these questions:
   What was the main reason you left your country?
   Were there other reasons?
   How did you choose where you would move?
   Who helped you in the new country?
   What kind of help did you need most?
   Did you have to learn a new language?
   How did your lifestyle change?
   Did it have an effect on family relationships?
   Add two questions of your own.
   Write up the interview as a newspaper article or make a panel presentation.
6. Describe and teach a simple game to your classmates.
7. Collect some magazine advertisements for athletic shoes (or any other product). What pictures and words do the advertisers use to make people want to buy the product? With another classmate, write your own advertisement for a product. Present it to your class.

If you enjoyed reading this story by Robert Olen Butler, we suggest that you read the other stories in his book, *A Good Scent From a Strange Mountain.* See the acknowledgements page for publishing information.

Unit
14

A FAMILY SUPPER
Kazuo Ishiguro

Japan

"I've come to believe now that there were no evil intentions in your mind," my father continued. "You were swayed by certain ... influences. Like so many others."

Unit
14

A FAMILY SUPPER
Kazuo Ishiguro

Japan

INTRODUCTION

This is the final unit in this book. We believe that most of you will be able to read this story without help from us. If you don't understand every word, don't worry. Just try to understand and appreciate the story. You might enjoy discussing it with your classmates.

A Family Supper

Kazuo Ishiguro

"A Family Supper" is a short story by Kazuo Ishiguro. Ishiguro was born in Japan, but at the age of six he went to live in England with his parents. He knows the two cultures and languages very well. In 1989 he won the Booker Prize in England for his book, *The Remains of the Day.*

Fugu is a fish caught off the Pacific shores of Japan. The fish has held a special significance for me ever since my mother died after eating one. The poison resides in the sex glands of the fish, inside two fragile bags. These bags must be removed with caution when preparing the fish, for any clumsiness will result in the poison leaking into the veins. Regrettably, it is not easy to tell whether or not this operation has been carried out successfully. The proof is, as it were, in the eating.

Fugu poisoning is hideously painful and almost always fatal. If the fish has been eaten during the evening, the victim is usually overtaken by pain during his sleep. He rolls about in agony for a few hours and is dead by morning. The fish became extremely popular in Japan after the war. Until stricter regulations were imposed, it was all the rage to perform the hazardous gutting operation in one's own kitchen, then to invite neighbors and friends round for the feast.

At the time of my mother's death, I was living in California. My relationship with my parents had become somewhat strained around that period and consequently I did not learn of the circumstances of her death until I returned to Tokyo two years later. Apparently, my mother had always refused to eat fugu, but on this particular occasion she had made an exception, having been invited by an old school friend whom she was anxious not to offend. It was my father who supplied me with the details as we drove from the airport to his house in the Kamakura district. When we finally arrived, it was nearing the end of a sunny autumn day.

"Did you eat on the plane?" my father asked. We were sitting on the tatami floor of his tearoom.

"They gave me a light snack."

"You must be hungry. We'll eat as soon as Kikuko arrives."

My father was formidable-looking man with a large stony jaw and furious black eyebrows. I think now, in retrospect, that he much resembled Chou En-lai, although he would not have cherished such a comparison, being particularly proud of the pure samurai blood that ran in the family. His general presence was not one that encouraged relaxed conversation; neither were things helped much by his odd way of stating each remark as if it were the concluding one. In fact, as I sat opposite him that afternoon, a boyhood memory of him came back of the time he had struck me several times around the head for "chattering like an old woman." Inevitably, our conversation since my arrival at the airport had been punctuated by long pauses.

"I'm sorry to hear about the firm," I said when neither of us had spoken for some time. He nodded gravely.

"In fact, the story didn't end there," he said. "After the firm's collapse, Watanabe killed himself. He didn't want to live with the disgrace."

"I see."

"We were partners for seventeen years. A man of principle and honor. I respected him very much."

"Will you go into business again?" I asked.

"I am...in retirement. I'm too old to involve myself in new ventures now. Business these days has become so different. Dealing with foreigners. Doing things their way. I don't understand how we've come to this. Neither did Watanabe." He sighed, "A fine man. A man of principle."

The tearoom looked out over the garden. From where I sat I could make out the ancient well that as a child I had believed to be haunted. It was just visible now through the thick foliage. The sun had sunk low and much of the garden had fallen into shadow.

"I'm glad in any case that you've decided to come back," my father said. "More than a short visit, I hope."

"I'm not sure what my plans will be."

"I, for one, am prepared to forget the past. Your mother, too, was always ready to welcome you back—upset as she was by your behavior."

"I appreciate your sympathy. As I say, I'm not sure what my plans are."

"I've come to believe now that there were no evil intentions in your mind," my father continued. "You were swayed by certain...influences. Like so many others."

"Perhaps we should forget it, as you suggest."

"As you will. More tea?"

Just then a girl's voice came echoing through the house.

"At last." My father rose to his feet. "Kikuko has arrived."

Despite our difference in years, my sister and I had always been close. Seeing me again seemed to make her excessively excited, and for a while she did nothing but giggle nervously. But she calmed down somewhat when my father started to question her about Osaka and her university. She answered him with short, formal replies. She in turn asked me a few questions, but she seemed inhibited by the fear that her questions might lead to awkward topics. After a while, the conversation had become even sparser than prior to Kikuko's arrival. Then my father stood up, saying: "I must attend to the supper. Please excuse me for being burdened by such matters. Kikuko will look after you."

My sister relaxed quite visibly once he had left the room. Within a few minutes, she was chatting freely about her friends in Osaka and about her classes at the university. Then quite suddenly she decided we should walk in the garden and went striding out onto the verandah. We put on some straw sandals that had been left along the verandah rail and stepped out into the garden. The light in the garden had grown very dim.

"I've been dying for a smoke for the last half hour," she said, lighting a cigarette.

"Then why didn't you smoke?"

She made a furtive gesture back toward the house, then grinned mischievously.

"Oh, I see," I said.

"Guess what? I've got a boyfriend now."

"Oh, yes?"

"Except I'm wondering what to do. I haven't made up my mind yet."

"Quite understandable."

"You see, he's making plans to go to America. He wants me to go with him as soon as I finish studying."

"I see. And you want to go to America?"

"If we go, we're going to hitchhike." Kikuko waved a thumb in front of my face. "People say it's dangerous, but I've done it in Osaka and it's fine."

"I see. So what is it that you're unsure about?"

We were following a narrow path that wound through the shrubs and finished by the old well. As we walked, Kikuko persisted in taking unnecessarily theatrical puffs on her cigarette.

"Well, I've got lots of friends in Osaka. I like it there. I'm not sure I want to leave them all behind just yet. And Suichi…I like him, but I'm not sure I want to spend so much time with him. Do you understand?"

"Oh, perfectly."

She grinned again, then skipped on ahead of me until she had reached the well. "Do you remember?" she said as I came walking up to her, "how you used to say this well was haunted?"

"Yes, I remember."

We both peered over the side.

"Mother always told me it was the old woman from the vegetable store you'd seen that night," she said. "But I never believed her and never came out here alone."

"Mother used to tell me that too. She even told me once the old woman had confessed to being the ghost. Apparently, she'd been taking a shortcut through our garden. I imagine she had some trouble clambering over these walls."

Kikuko gave a giggle. She then turned back to the wall, casting her gaze about the garden.

"Mother never really blamed you, you know," she said, in a new voice. I remained silent. "She always used to say to me how it was their fault, hers and Father's, for not bringing you up correctly. She used to tell me how much more careful they'd been with me, and that's why I was so good." She looked up and the mischievous grin had returned to her face. "Poor Mother," she said.

"Yes. Poor mother."

"Are you going back to California?"

"I don't know. I'll have to see."

"What happened...to her? To Vicki?"

"That's all finished with," I said. "There's nothing much left for me now in California."

"Do you think I ought to go there?"

"Why not? I don't know. You'd probably like it." I glanced toward the house. "Perhaps we'd better go in soon. Father might need a hand with the supper."

But my sister was once more peering down into the well. "I can't see any ghosts," she said. Her voice echoed a little.

"Is Father very upset with his firm collapsing?"

"Don't know. You never can tell with Father." Then suddenly she straightened up and turned to me. "Did he tell you about old Watanabe? What he did?

"I heard he committed suicide."

"Well, that wasn't all. He took his whole family with him. His wife and his two little girls."

"Oh, yes?"

"Those two beautiful little girls. He turned on the gas while they were all asleep. Then he cut his stomach with a meat knife."

"Yes, Father was telling me that Watanabe was a man of principle."

"Sick." My sister turned to the well.

"Careful. You'll fall right in."

"I can't see any ghost," she said. "You were lying to me all that time." "But I never said it lived down the well."

"Where is it then?"

We both looked around at the trees and shrubs. The daylight had almost gone. Eventually I pointed to a small clearing some ten yards away.

"Just there I saw it. Just there."

We stared at the spot.

"What did it look like?"

"I couldn't see very well. It was dark."

"But you must have seen something."

"It was an old woman. She was just standing there, watching me."

We kept staring at the spot as if mesmerized.

"She was wearing a white kimono," I said. "Some of her hair came undone. It was blowing around a little."

Kikuko pushed her elbow against my arm. "Oh, be quiet. You're trying to frighten me all over again." She trod on the remains of her cigarette, then for a brief moment stood regarding it with a perplexed expression. She kicked some pine needles over it, then once more displayed her grin. "Let's see if supper is ready," she said.

We found my father in the kitchen. He gave us a quick glance, then carried on with what he was doing.

"Father's become quite a chef since he's had to manage on his own," Kikuko said with a laugh.

He turned and looked at my sister coldly. "Hardly a skill I'm proud of," he said. "Kikuko come and help."

For some moments my sister did not move. Then she stepped forward and took an apron hanging from a drawer.

"Just these vegetables need cooking now," he said to her. "The rest just needs watching." Then he looked up and regarded me strangely for some seconds. "I expect you want to look around the house," he said eventually. He put down the chopsticks he had been holding. "It's a long time since you've seen it."

As we left the kitchen I glanced towards Kikuko, but her back was turned.

"She's a good girl," my father said.

I followed my father from room to room. I had forgotten how large the house was. A panel would slide open and another room would appear. But the rooms were all startlingly empty. In one of the rooms the lights did not come on, and we stared at the stark walls and tatami in the pale light that came from the windows.

"This house is too large for a man to live in alone," my father said. "I don't have much use for these rooms now."

But eventually my father opened the door to a room packed full of books and papers. There were flowers in vases and pictures on the walls. Then I noticed something on a low table in the corner of the room. I came nearer and saw it was a plastic model of a battleship, the kind constructed by children. It had been placed on some newspaper; scattered around it were assorted pieces of gray plastic.

My father gave a laugh. He came to the table and picked up the model.

"Since the firm folded," he said "I have a little more time on my hands." He laughed again, rather strangely. For a moment his face looked almost gentle. "A little more time."

"That seems odd," I said. "You were always so busy."

"Too busy, perhaps." He looked at me with a small smile. "Perhaps I should have been a more attentive father."

I laughed. He went on contemplating his battleship. Then he looked up. "I hadn't meant to tell you this, but perhaps it's better that I do. It's my belief that your mother's death was no accident. She had many worries. And some disappointments."

We both gazed at the plastic battleship.

"Surely," I said eventually, "my mother didn't expect me to live here forever."

"Obviously you don't see. You don't see how it is for some parents. Not only must they lose their children, they must lose them to things they don't understand." He spun the battleship in his fingers. "These little gunboats here could have been better glued, don't you think?"

"Perhaps. I think it looks fine."

"During the war I spent some time on a ship rather like this. But my ambition was always the air force. I figured it like this: If your ship was struck by the enemy, all you could do was struggle in the water hoping for a lifeline. But in an airplane—well, there was always the final weapon." He put the model back onto the table. "I don't suppose you believe in war."

"Not particularly."

He cast an eye around the room. "Supper should be ready by now," he said. "You must be hungry."

Supper was waiting in a dimly lit room next to the kitchen. The only source of light was a big lantern that hung over the table, casting the rest of the room in shadow. We bowed to each other before starting the meal.

There was little conversation. When I made some polite comment about the food, Kikuko giggled a little. Her earlier nervousness seemed to have returned to her. My father did not speak for several minutes. Finally he said:

"It must feel strange for you being back in Japan."

"Yes, it is a little strange."

"Already, perhaps, you regret leaving America."

"A little. Not so much. I didn't leave behind much. Just some empty rooms."

"I see."

I glanced across the table. My father's face looked stony and forbidding in the half-light. We ate on in silence.

Then my eye caught something at the back of the room. At first I continued eating, then my hands became still. The others noticed and looked at me. I went on gazing into the darkness past my father's shoulder.

"Who is that? In that photograph there?"

"Which photograph?" My father turned slightly, trying to follow my gaze.

"The lowest one. The woman in the white kimono."

My father put down his chopsticks. He looked first at the photograph, then at me.

"Your mother." His voice had become very hard. "Can't you recognize your own mother?"

"My mother. You see, it's dark. I can't see it very well."

No one spoke for a few seconds, then Kikuko rose to her feet. She took the photograph down from the wall, came back to the table, and gave it to me.

"She looks a lot older," I said.

"It was taken shortly before her death," said my father.

"It was the dark. I couldn't see very well."

I looked up and noticed my father holding out a hand. I gave him the photograph. He looked at it intently, then held it toward Kikuko. Obediently, my sister rose to her feet once more and returned the picture to the wall.

There was a large pot left unopened at the center of the table. When Kikuko had seated herself again, my father reached forward and lifted the lid. A cloud of steam rose up and curled toward the lantern. He pushed the pot a little toward me.

"You must be hungry," he said. One side of his face had fallen into shadow.

"Thank you." I reached forward with my chopsticks. The steam was almost scalding. "What is it?"

"Fish."

"It smells very good."

In the soup were strips of fish that had curled almost into balls. I picked one out and brought it to my bowl.

"Help yourself. There's plenty."

"Thank you." I took a little more, then pushed the pot toward my father. I watched him take several pieces to his bowl. Then we both watched as Kikuko served herself.

My father bowed slightly. "You must be hungry," he said again. He took some fish to his mouth and started to eat. Then, I too, chose a piece and put it in my mouth. It felt soft, quite fleshy against my tongue.

The three of us ate in silence. Several minutes went by. My father lifted the lid and once more steam rose up. We all reached forward and helped ourselves.

"Here," I said to my father, "you have this last piece."

"Thank you."

When we had finished the meal, my father stretched out his arms and yawned with an air of satisfaction. "Kikuko," he said, "prepare a pot of tea, please."

My sister looked at him, then left the room without comment. My father stood up.

"Let's retire to the other room. It's rather warm in here."

I got to my feet and followed him into the tearoom. The large sliding windows had been left open, bringing a breeze from the garden. For a while we sat in silence.

"Father," I said finally.

"Yes?"

"Kikuko tells me Watanabe-san took his whole family with him."

My father lowered his eyes and nodded. For some moments he seemed deep in thought. "Watanabe was very devoted to his work," he said at last. "The collapse of the firm was a great blow to him. I fear it must have weakened his judgement."

"You think what he did . . . it was a mistake?"

"Why, of course. Do you see it otherwise?"

"No, no. Of course not."

"There are other things besides work," my father said.

"Yes."

We fell silent again. The sound of locusts came in from the garden. I looked out into the darkness. The well was no longer visible.

"What do you think you will do now?" my father asked. "Will you stay in Japan for a while?"

"To be honest, I hadn't thought that far ahead."

"If you wish to stay here, I mean here in this house, you would be very welcome. That is, if you don't mind living with an old man."

"Thank you. I'll have to think about it."

I gazed out once more into the darkness.

"But of course," said my father, "this house is so dreary now. You'll no doubt return to America before long."

"Perhaps. I don't know yet."

"No doubt you will."

For some time my father seemed to be studying the back of his hands. Then he looked up and sighed.

"Kikuko is due to complete her studies next spring," he said. "Perhaps she will want to come home then. She's a good girl."

"Perhaps she will."

"Things will improve then."

"Yes, I'm sure they will."

We fell silent once more, waiting for Kikuko to bring the tea.

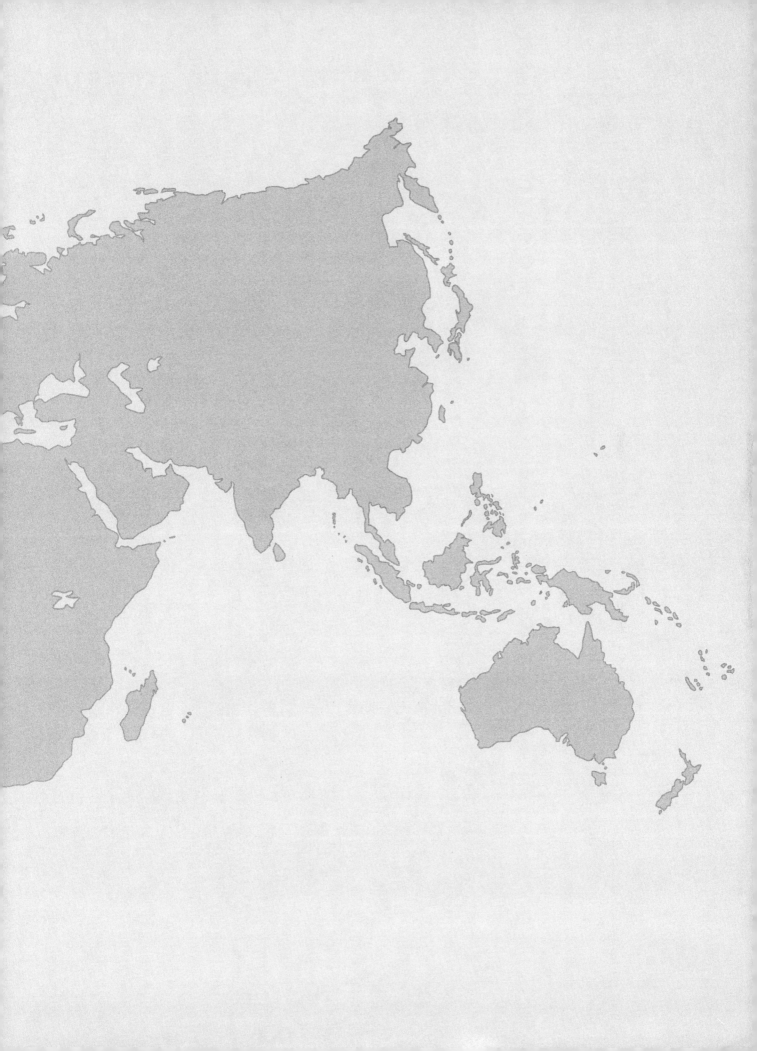

EXPLORING WHAT YOU READ

TOPICS FOR DISCUSSIONS OR ESSAYS

Following are topics designed to deepen your understanding of the stories. Some of the topics ask you to compare (describe what is similar) and contrast (describe what is different) in the stories; others ask for your opinion. Refer back to the stories as you respond. Remember, the opinions you form are your own, and you are invited to express them freely.

1. Compare and contrast the lives and personalities of any two of these characters: Amina ("Amina," Unit 1), Sister ("Spring Love," Unit 5), Uma ("Fasting, Feasting," Unit 6), Lucy ("Poor Visitor," Unit 7), Mita ("Clothes," Unit 9), or Adah ("Second Class Citizen," Unit 10).

2. Compare and contrast the information that the narrators of Unit 2 ("Every Light in the House Burnin'") and Unit 3 ("Family Album") give about their parents. Then compare and contrast the writing styles of the authors.

3. In Unit 5 ("Spring Love") and Unit 4 ("The Visit"), the central characters feel a lot of pain. Compare and contrast their situations.

4. In what ways does the European presence change the lives of local people in Units 11 and 12? In your opinion, are these changes positive or negative? Explain your answer.

5. Describe how traditions influence the lives and decisions of the characters in two or more of the stories in Units 1, 6, 8, 9, 10, 11, 12, or 13.

6. Write about your favorite story and explain what you especially like about it.

7. Write about your least favorite story and explain why you dislike it.

8. In general, are the characters and situations in *Views and Voices* easy or difficult for you to understand? Explain your answer and give examples.

9. Write a letter to the authors of the book describing how *Views and Voices* was helpful or not helpful to you. Email or mail your letter to the publisher (see page iv for address information).

10. Visit **www.miniature-earth.com** (make sure that Flash is loaded on your computer and that the sound is on). The short film contained on this site presents statistics on world economics, literacy, health, and welfare by proportionally reducing the earth's 6 billion inhabitants to a small village of 100 people. Does the information provided in the film have an impact on your reading of the stories in *Views and Voices?* How are the authors contained in this book representative and unrepresentative of the global population? How did watching the film make you feel?

Answer Key

Unit 1

VOCABULARY

1. embrace
2. despair
3. blush
4. twinkling
5. moan
6. catastrophe
7. disgrace
8. murmured
9. distressed

LANGUAGE

1. eager for
2. pressing for
3. burst into
4. reverting to
5. turned out to be

Unit 2

VOCABULARY

1. disciplining
2. affectionate
3. proper
4. demanded
5. embarrassed
6. properly
7. ain't
8. furiously
9. contact
10. suitable

LANGUAGE

1. warm up
2. took in
3. pick up
4. born and bred
5. wash up
6. late shift
7. early riser
8. propped up
9. aimed at
10. watch the clock

Unit 3

VOCABULARY

1. proved
2. natural
3. tossed
4. preached
5. crop
6. mayor
7. tore
8. inheritance
9. chop

LANGUAGE

1. dreamed of
2. from all around
3. smiling at
4. step on
5. bring (his dreams) down to size

Unit 4

VOCABULARY

1. remain
2. dared
3. wrapped
4. hero
5. supposed to
6. pretend
7. upset
8. adventures
9. cheerful
10. managed
11. inventing

LANGUAGE

1. bend down
2. throw up
3. put down
4. wide open
5. play with
6. get over
7. shake your head
8. come back
9. Turn off
10. fell out

Unit 5

EXPLORING

VOCABULARY

1. stage
2. urge
3. status, fame
4. crashed
5. approving, encourage
6. ambitions
7. eagerly
8. seek
9. preach
10. limit

LANGUAGE

1. snow drift
2. out of proportion
3. spying on
4. caked with, faded into
5. aim at

Unit 6

EXPLORING

VOCABULARY

1. evidence
2. inspect
3. protested
4. disgrace
5. confident
6. authorities
7. sequence

LANGUAGE

1. launch (a man) into space
2. step into
3. welled up
4. lack of interest
5. double strength
6. sloshed out
7. wound up
8. linked arms
9. slipped into
10. vouch for

Unit 7

VOCABULARY

1. blame
2. behind (his) back
3. routine
4. situation
5. sincere
6. regard
7. solid
8. dissolves
9. precious
10. familiar

LANGUAGE

1. greeting cards
2. engage (them) in conversation
3. draw attention
4. occurred to
5. In general
6. singled (her) out
7. sum up
8. taken (me) for granted
9. millstone around my neck
10. behind my back

Unit 8

EXPLORING

VOCABULARY

1. announcement
2. background
3. grateful
4. complain
5. satisfactory
6. shame
7. properly
8. discreetly
9. question
10. self-respecting

LANGUAGE

1. come up
2. foreign land
3. proposed marriage
4. pointed (it) out, brought (it) up
5. go ahead
6. tell the truth
7. burst out
8. laugh at
9. spat out
10. at one sitting

Unit 9

EXPLORING

VOCABULARY

1. concept
2. ashamed
3. straighten
4. spine
5. widow
6. shivering
7. fragrant
8. arguments
9. scold
10. shattered

LANGUAGE

1. nodded agreement
2. back and forth
3. spit (it) out
4. running at a loss
5. graveyard shift
6. burglar alarm
7. hired help

Unit 10

VOCABULARY

1. pleaded
2. guidance
3. subject matter
4. permit
5. attempt
6. opinion
7. generations
8. barely tolerate
9. challenge
10. bothered

LANGUAGE

1. at random
2. in pain
3. heroic conquest
4. smack his lips
5. the last straw
6. stepping stones
7. For the time being
8. ended up

Unit 11

EXPLORING

VOCABULARY

1. evil
2. power
3. attracted
4. savage blows
5. disagreement
6. approach
7. victory
8. confident
9. furious
10. abandon

LANGUAGE

1. evil spirits
2. in sympathy
3. good riddance
4. in vain
5. wipe out
6. dumping ground
7. right senses
8. sprang to his feet
9. set limits
10. cold shudder

Unit 12

EXPLORING

VOCABULARY

1. drought
2. produce
3. severe
4. starvation
5. ancestors
6. strain
7. tragedies
8. protect
9. insects
10. purchase

LANGUAGE

1. stamps his foot/feet
2. fled away
3. in season
4. spring up
5. curled up
6. in despair
7. cloud of sorrow
8. haunted by
9. In desperation
10. lose their heads

Unit 13

VOCABULARY

1. bitter
2. slam
3. capture
4. grabbed
5. confused
6. glanced
7. admitted
8. decades
9. Crickets
10. ruined

LANGUAGE

1. refugee center
2. civilian clothes
3. hanging around
4. hard struggle
5. rice paddies
6. chemical engineer
7. root for
8. crack a corny joke
9. at best
10. stripped off

ACQUISITIONS EDITOR: Aaron Berman

LEAD CONTENT EDITOR: Sarah Tanke

CONTENT AND PRODUCTION EDITORS:

Jamie Ann Cross and Raissa Nina Burns

DESIGN: Regina Schindler Rowland, Creative Director and Designer

Civiane Chung, Designer and Production Artist

Claudia Müller, Designer, Production Artist and Illustrator

Alta Book Center Publishers

14 Adrian Court, Burlingame, California 94010 USA

Phone: 800 ALTA/ESL • 650.692.1285—International

Fax: 800 ALTA/FAX • 650.692.4654—International

Email: info@altaesl.com • Website: www.altaesl.com

ISBN 1-882483-87-1

Library of Congress Control Number: 2001095446